A New Spirit in Architecture

PETER EISENMAN, KOIZUMI LIGHTING THEATRE, TOKYO
This project will be extensively featured in a forthcoming issue

THE WILSON PARTNERSHIP, BLACKBURN HOUSE, LONDON

Architectural Design
Edited by Andreas C Papadakis

A New Spirit in Architecture

OMA, CHECKPOINT CHARLIE, PAINTING BY ZOE ZENGHELIS, 1987, OIL ON CANVAS
See pp48-55 for built project

ACADEMY EDITIONS • LONDON

Acknowledgements

Publications relevant to this issue
Carter Wiseman, *The Architecture of I M Pei*, published by Abrams, New York, and Thames and Hudson, London
Heinrich Klotz, *Zamp Kelp, Haus Rucker Co, Bauten und Projekte zu Architektur und Medialität Werkübersicht*, published by
Zentrum für Kunst- und Medientechnologie, Karlsruhe
William S Saunders, *Modern Architecture Photographs by Ezra Stoller*, Abrams, New York

Photo Credits
p1: Peter Aaron of Esto; p6: photograph courtesy of The German Architecture Museum in Frankfurt; pp22-29: Christian
Kandzia of Behnisch and Partners; pp30-37: Hiroyuki Hirai and Tadao Ando; p38-49: all photographs supplied by Philippe
Starck; p50-55: Michel Claus and EJ Ouwerkerk; p56-71: interview by Vivian Constantinopoulos; photographs: pp 56, 58, 65,
66, 67, 68, 69 (left) Hélène Binet; pp 59, 62, 69 (right) Richard Bryant; pp 60, 63, 64, 70 John Freeman; p72-79: all photographs
supplied by Zamp Kelp; p80-85: all Ezra Stoller photographs reproduced by permission of Erica Stoller; text by William S
Saunders extracted from his essay in the book (see above); p92-96: Christian Norberg-Schultz *The New Tradition* was first given
as a lecture in Zurich, 1990

EDITOR
Dr Andreas C Papadakis

EDITORIAL OFFICES: 42 LEINSTER GARDENS, LONDON W2 3AN TELEPHONE: 071-402 2141
CONSULTANTS: Catherine Cooke, Dennis Crompton, Terry Farrell, Kenneth Frampton, Charles Jencks,
Heinrich Klotz, Leon Krier, Robert Maxwell, Demetri Porphyrios, Colin Rowe, Derek Walker.
EDITORIAL TEAM: Maggie Toy (House Editor), Vivian Constantinopoulos, Helen Castle
DESIGNED BY:Andrea Bettella, Mario Bettella SUBSCRIPTIONS MANAGER: Mira Joka

First published in Great Britain in 1991 by *Architectural Design*
an imprint of the
ACADEMY GROUP LTD, 7 HOLLAND STREET, LONDON W8 4NA
ISBN: 1-85490-092-7 (UK)

Architectural Design Profile 89 is published as part of *Architectural Design* Vol 61 1-2/1991
Published in the United States of America by
ST MARTIN'S PRESS, 175 FIFTH AVENUE, NEW YORK 10010
ISBN: 0-312-06502-7 (USA)

Printed and bound in Singapore

MAKOTO SEI WATANABE, THE DRAMA OF EXPERIENCE

Contents

Architectural Design Profile No. 89

A New Spirit in Architecture

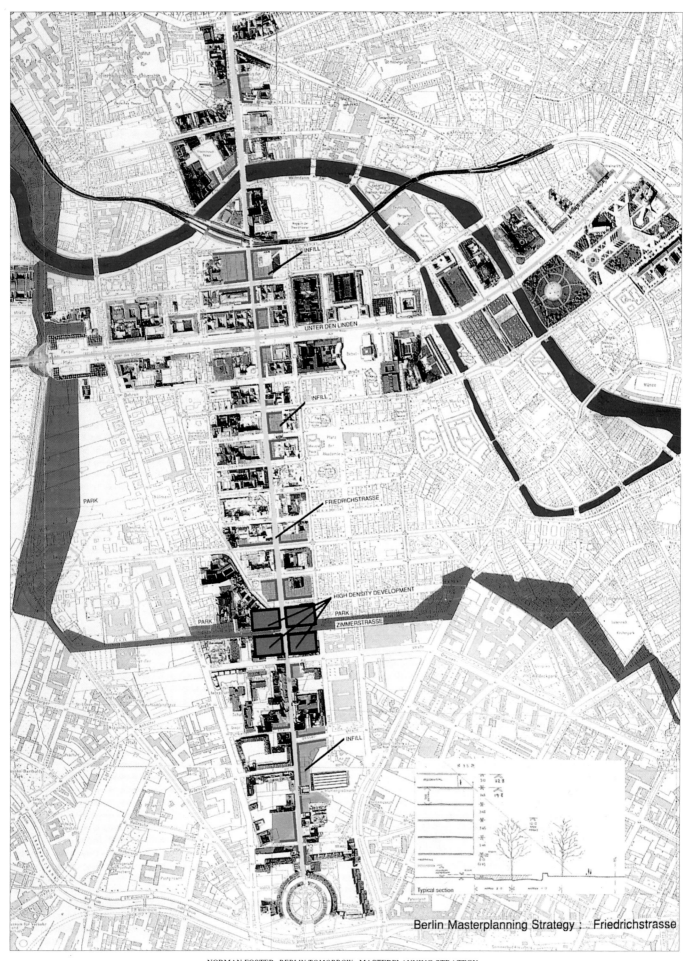

INFILL

INFILL

FRIEDRICHSTRASSE

HIGH DENSITY DEVELOPMENT

PARK

ZIMMERSTRASSE

PARK

PARK

INFILL

UNTER DEN LINDEN

Typical section

Berlin Masterplanning Strategy : Friedrichstrasse

NORMAN FOSTER, *BERLIN TOMORROW*, MASTERPLANNING STRATEGY
This and other *Berlin Tomorrow* schemes will be extensively featured in a forthcoming issue

EDITORIAL

Norman Foster's submission for the *Berlin Tomorrow* Ideas Competition reinforces the theme of this issue, and is a timely reminder of the possibilities that are open to architects. This presentation is especially interesting when compared with the Checkpoint Charlie Housing project. Following the almost total demolition of the Berlin Wall, this scheme by Elia Zenghelis and Matthias Sauerbruch has been completed just in time to perpetuate a name now relegated to the history books. While certain design decisions, such as set-back dimensions and sectional zoning to separate between military and civilian users, were made in direct response to the famous crossing nearby, the design retains its own personality, even in the absence of its forbidding neighbour.

Many of the projects presented here only reached the press as proposals a short while ago, and their rapid realisation shows the speed with which things are happening in architecture today. These include commissions that run the gamut from the residential scale of the Blackburn house to the monumentality of the Louvre expansion, by I M Pei, which has been the most widely discussed Grand Project in Paris since Bernard Tschumi's La Villette. We have been given an opportunity to take an inside view of Carter Wiseman's recent book on I M Pei, published by Harry N Abrams. His chapter on the Louvre graphically conveys the extent of the controversy surrounding Pei's much needed addition, as well as the degree of conviction that was necessary on the part of both the architect and the client to see it through.

We also trace the recent progress of other architects such as Peter Wilson, Günter Behnisch, Philippe Starck, Zamp Kelp and Hani Rashid. Peter Wilson originally raised some eyebrows with his designs for bridges over the Thames that have never proceeded past the conceptual stage, and it is now very exciting to see what he has been able to achieve with a supportive client. His Blackburn house is virtually invisible from the street, turning inward to provide a visually and spatially supportive framework for the clients' collection of contemporary furniture. In this refined setting, each detail takes on a heightened significance, because the furniture, and not the architecture, has always been intended to take pride of place. Günter Behnisch, whose Hysolar Factory in Stuttgart was first presented by Academy at an Exhibition called '21 Canonical Architects' that ran concurrently with the Symposium on Pluralism held in Frankfurt in 1989, has recently completed the last in a series of 13 museums commissioned by that city, which have mostly been built along the Schaumainkai. His ingenious design for the Postal Museum shows how the same aesthetic sensibilities that were subjected to budgetary restrictions alone in Stuttgart have here been adapted to a more confined and historically sensitive urban site. By turning to a partially underground solution, Behnisch has been able to not only satisfy both the present and anticipated spatial requirements of the Museum, but has also managed to relate to the complicated context around it. The architect, in doing so, has saved many full-grown trees that would have otherwise been destroyed. New work by Philippe Starck is also indicative of his own professional growth and increasing visibility in the public eye, since for quite some time his main claim to fame was a small café in Paris. His special kind of theatricality has found the perfect outlet in Japan, where it has captured the imagination of a wide range of corporate clients. As has been the case with several Western architects who have found the stylistic freedom of Tokyo to be extremely refreshing, Starck has capitalised upon the Japanese attitude that innovative form is now fashionable. His forms, however, seem to cross over the fine line that has separated the metaphorical from the bizarre and surreal, and he shows a decided preference for organic, curved surfaces. Starck has single-handedly managed to open up a new front on what appears to be a frenetic international campaign to discover a more meaningful, or at least more attention-getting architecture of signs, and the futuristic direction that he has taken has definitely set him apart in this category.

The work of Hani Rashid, who recalls Daniel Libeskind in his preference for an architecture that is accompanied by a written narrative is a confirmation, if any were needed, that the age of information has really arrived. Rashid's conjunctive pairing of architecture with text is a further indication of current movement away from the idea of establishing semiotic or linguistic comparisons with tectonic elements, towards the consideration of the combination of the parts of architecture as a language all of their own. By alluding, in his text, to the 'ignominious machines' that now produce 'Hygienic architecture for the civilised', Rashid also raises the issue of the proper place for technology today. Where Modernism may have attempted to rely heavily upon it as the basis of its philosophy, Rashid seems to represent a direction that shifts its reliance to the abstractions and representations of language instead.

In his article called 'The New Tradition', Christian Norberg-Schulz addresses this same issue from a different direction, by asking how, or even if, it is possible to derive an architecture that both reflects the dynamism of modernity, and yet answers to what he perceives to be the need for a 'timeless' built environment.

In his clarification of this concept of timelessness, however, Norberg-Schulz uses a Modern, rather than vernacular exegesis, quoting Kepes, Le Corbusier, Giedion, Heidegger, and Kahn, among others. Noting one of Kahn's favourite pedagogical tests of timelessness, that any valid work of architecture should convey what 'has always been', Norberg-Schulz goes on to relate this to his view of the need to respect the diversity existing in the world today. Only then, he believes, may we leave what he calls 'the crisis of Modernism' behind, and move on to a New Tradition.

The single spirit that seems to unite both writings and buildings is a persistent questioning of the direction that contemporary architecture should be taking today, with the variety of the answers showing that pluralism is still alive and well in all respects.   [*Ed*]

I M PEI

THE BATTLE OF THE PYRAMID

*I M Pei has designed some of this century's most contro-
versial and powerful buildings; for more than forty years he
and his firm have made major contributions to world
architecture. Whilst Pei is widely known as a Modernist, his
aesthetic cannot be reduced to or defined by any particular
style, his work eluding such simple categorisation. In the
Modernist tradition he remains devoted to rigorous geometry and to the use of simple forms. The result of his
studies may not resemble his neighbours', but it is almost
always calculated to fit into a larger urban or landscape
composition. The pyramid he designed for the Louvre in
Paris is a clever solution to the problem of extending an
exemplary traditional building with one which has modern
technological requirements. Here we present the account
by Carter Wiseman of how the project came to be realised.*

In May of 1988, François Mitterrand was running for a
second term as president of France. On the night of the
voting, as was his custom at the end of a campaign, he
chose to await the results at a quiet inn outside Paris. This
time, the innkeeper had prepared a special treat in anticipation of his customer's all-but certain victory. When the
reports indicated that Mitterrand was securely ahead, the
innkeeper brought in his creation. It was a cake, but there
was nothing unusual about that. The surprise was the
complicated little structure made of icing on the top. Rather
than a French flag or the Arc de Triomphe, as might have
been expected, it was, unmistakably, a pyramid.[1]

The inspiration for the miniature ornament was the 71-
foot-high glass structure that Pei had recently erected as
the new entrance to the ambitious renovation of the Louvre
museum in Paris. Mitterrand had selected Pei personally
for the job five years before, and together they had weath-
ered a firestorm of criticism to get it done. Under the
circumstances, the fact that a work of architecture should
have come to symbolise a political triumph was only fitting.
'At the base of all politics,' Mitterrand had declared after
visiting the construction site of the pyramid two months
earlier, 'is the politics of culture.'

Perhaps only in France could a head of state make such a
pronouncement without risk of pretension. For in France,
culture – especially as it is expressed in architecture –
remains inseparable from national pride. The country's
kings for centuries raised monuments to embody the
power of the state and after the Second World War the
tradition was continued with unflagging élan. Georges
Pompidou commissioned the national arts centre in the
Beaubourg district of Paris, and his successor, Valéry
Giscard d'Estaing, redeveloped the disused markets of Les
Halles and transformed the old Orsay railway station into
an art museum. 'Louis XIV had his Versailles,' observed a
French member Of the Pei team. 'President Mitterrand has
the Louvre.'

For Mitterrand's architect, the above ground portion of
the Louvre project (the part that caused most of the
controversy) was one of the smaller buildings he had done.
But by the time the entire undertaking was finished, it had
become the single most demanding – and rewarding –
commission he had ever received. It involved not only
architecture, but art, politics, planning, diplomacy, and
sheer grit in a unique admixture. It subjected him to
unprecedented strains and gave him his greatest victory. 'It
was the most important project of my life,' said Pei shortly
after the building was opened to the public. 'It's unnerving
if I look back on it.'

If French heads of state have dedicated themselves to
great building programmes for their personal gloire, they
have also been serving a public trust. Unlike the United
States, France does not leave its cultural monuments in the
hands of private philanthropists the state is by far the
major patron. And by the early 1980s, no French cultural
landmark was in greater need of patronage than the Louvre.
Its royal builders had never intended it to be a museum.
Indeed, the Minister of Finance had occupied roughly half
the building since the 1870s, and the last important work
on the building had been done in the 1880s. Since then, it
had come to sustain an annual flood of nearly three million
visitors, who had to negotiate its confusing layout and vast
galleries with a minimum of modern museum aids and
amenities. (There were, for example, only two bathrooms
and a meagre cafeteria available to the public.) According
to some Parisians, the most frequently asked question
about the Louvre was how to find the front door.

If visitors were suffering, so were the works of art. While
the Louvre's collection had grown over the centuries to
include hundreds of thousands of items, only a fraction of
them could be displayed in its limited gallery space; the
rest were in storage or on loan to other institutions. And
while most modern museums set aside approximately 50
percent of their interiors for non-gallery use the Louvre's
need for gallery space left only ten percent of the museums
square footage for such critical functions as administration, storage, conservation and research. Museum people
were fond of referring to one of the world's greatest
museums as 'a theatre without a backstage' and 'a masterwork
of incoherence.'

Despite its lamentable condition, the Louvre's age and
prominence had long been good enough to make it an
obligatory tourist attraction. But since the completion in
1977 of Pompidou's Beaubourg cultural centre, the new
building had snatched first place from the Eiffel Tower by a
considerable margin. Of those who continued to come to
the Louvre, only 30 percent were French and only ten
percent Parisians, an embarrassing tally for such a national treasure.

Shortly after Mitterrand's election as president in 1981,

*Although the public
furore that greeted his
plan for the Louvre
focused almost entirely
on the design of the
pyramid, Pei approached
the project from the start
as a planning problem. In
addition to reordering the
museum, he intended to
reanimate what had
become a back-water in
central Paris.*

Having decided to put the ceremonial main space underground, the architect countered the potential for a 'subway station' effect with light-coloured stone and a frankly theatrical staircase.

the combination of the Louvre's institutional decay and the resulting cultural loss of face began to have an especially strong impact on his new Minister of Culture, Jack Lang. 'I would pass by the Louvre every day,' Lang said. 'I thought how awful was the presence of all the cars and buses, how stupid that the Minister of Finance occupies part of the Louvre. So I wrote a note to the president asking why not a Grand Louvre, without the Finance Ministry there. It could be a beautiful symbol. Culture will win against finance.'[2]

Mitterrand was impressed, and in September of 1981, he decided to act, declaring at his first presidential press conference that the Ministry of Finance, which occupied the Louvre's northern, or Richelieu, wing along the Rue de Rivoli, would be moving to other quarters and that its space would be turned over to the museum. The goal was to turn the L-shaped museum into a larger and more workable U-shaped one, something the museum's administrators had proposed often in the past but had never been able to accomplish.

The decision to convert the Richelieu wing meant that the entire Louvre could be reorganised. But tampering with the building was a daunting proposition, especially because so much more than architecture was involved. Indeed, the building had long ago become a semi-sacred place for the French, embodying as it did so much of the history and spirit of the nation. It was begun around 1190 as a fortified castle by King Philippe Auguste in a forest where wolves once roamed. In 1365, Charles V transformed the fortress into his royal residence. François I later raised the fortress and erected on the site a new group of buildings, which were added to by Henry IV (who ordered the construction of the gallery along the Seine), Louis XIV (who turned the Louvre into an institution for advanced study), Napoleon I, and Napoleon III.

Over the years, parts of the complex had served variously as barracks, prison, academy, administrative offices, and art school. In 1793, the revolutionary Convention decided to use one of the galleries to exhibit the royal art collections to the public, and so was born the idea of the Louvre as a museum. Thus the building has always meant much more to France than say, the National Gallery has to the United States. It is almost as if the White House, the Capitol, and the Lincoln Memorial had all been combined with the gallery in a single structure.

When Mitterrand took office, he had already had several *grands projets* in mind. Ultimately, they would include an enormous office building, known as the Grande Arche de la Défense, behind the Arc de Triomphe, the multi-purpose Parc de la Villette on the northern edge of Paris and an opera house to take over the functions of Charles Garnier's 1875 triumph of guilded excess. Considered together, these and Mitterrand's other undertakings would make him the most ambitious builder in modern French history. But the Louvre was the first of his projects, and clearly the one that mattered most.

Pei's first contact with the French president took place on December 11, 1981. He had recently been awarded a gold medal by the French academy of architecture and was invited to meet personally with Mitterrand. During the meeting, which took place at the Elysée Palace, Mitterrand told Pei that he had visited the East building and had admired an earlier, ill-fated Pei proposal (done with Araldo Cossutta) for the office complex at La Défense. He expressed his hope that Pei might participate in some of the projects he was planning for Paris. Pei replied as gracefully as he could that he had no time to enter competitions. To

which Mitterrand answered, 'Well, we are flexible'. There was no mention of the Louvre.

Not long afterwards, Mitterrand began assembling a team to oversee the architecture projects he was contemplating. For the Louvre, the president turned to a leathery civil servant named Emile Biasini. A veteran of 15 years in the French colonies in West Africa, Biasini had been a cabinet member under André Malraux, De Gaulle's Minister of Culture and a director of French national television. With close cropped grey hair and a nose that reflected the rigours of the rugby he had played as a youth, he radiated a compelling sturdiness, a quality he would need as Mitterrand's right hand on the Louvre. In the fall of 1983, he was given the title of president of the Etablissement Public du Grande Louvre, the government agency set up to handle the job. His first task was to look into the selection of an architect. 'I wanted someone capable of respecting history, but innovative enough to attack anew', he said.

Biasini was well aware of the hazards of his assignment. Indeed, in 1665, when Louis XIV had invited Bernini – the most celebrated architect, sculptor and designer of his time – to do for the Louvre what he had for Saint Peter's in Rome, the Italian, flamboyant proposal ran afoul of Louis' finance minister, Colbert, and the leading French architects, and he was sent home. No less a talent than François Mansart, probably the greatest of all French architects, had had 15 projects for redesigning the palace rejected. The Louvre is 'part of the cultural patrimony of the world', said Biasini of the building he was charged with renovating. But, he added, 'if it was to continue as a Museum, it was absolutely necessary to do something. The Louvre was in a grave condition. It was the world's most miserable museum'.

The common practice in such a situation was to set up an architectural competition. To educate himself about possible candidates, Biasini spent nine months touring museums in Europe and the United States. Among his stops was Pei's East building, which made a strong impression. 'I asked many people which architect they would choose,' Biasini said. 'Pei was on every list'. As a Chinese, he had 'an understanding of an ancient civilisation' and, as an American, 'he had a taste for the modern'.

Biasini subsequently asked a friend of Pei's who was living in Paris, an expatriate Chinese painter named Zao Wou-ki, to introduce them. Pei and his wife shortly thereafter were visiting Paris, and a meeting was arranged at the Hotel Raphael, which was much favoured by publicity-shy luminaries for its discreet location on the Avenue Kléber. Biasini told Pei that Mitterrand had asked him to make recommendations about the Louvre and that two or three other architects were being considered, but that he himself had been impressed by Pei's work. Pei reiterated that he no longer participated in competitions.

A few weeks later, Biasini called Pei in New York to say that he was coming to the United States and would like to meet again. Pei agreed, and at their meeting Biasini asked him if he would accept the Louvre project if he were offered. According to Biasini, Mitterrand had concluded that, despite the danger of the precedent, the Louvre was too important an enterprise to leave to the uncertainties of competition. Pei said that 'it was probably impossible' to alter the Louvre, but that he would look into it. He would have to study the possibility of doing such a thing before responding officially, and he thought he would need at least four months. The loss of the La Défense project had been painful, he pointed out, and he was not about to

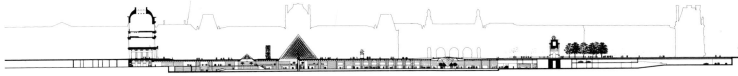

Pei meeting with François Mitterrand in June of 1983. The President of the Republic felt so strongly about the importance of the Louvre that he abandoned the customary practice of holding a competition to select an architect.

Pei and Mitterrand on the construction site with Emile Biasini (centre), the determined civil servant who backed the plan through all its crises.

Computers were used to generate drawings that helped the architect assess the impact of the pyramid on the semi-sacred monument.

embark on another effort in Paris – and especially not this one – without proper preparation.

Biasini agreed, and Pei subsequently made three trips to Paris, staying for periods of a week to ten days at the elegant Hotel Crillon, on the Place de la Concorde, a short walk from the museum. He read widely on the history of the Louvre and the history of France and was given a *laissez-passer* to go anywhere he wanted in the Louvre. Lest Pei's real mission become known, only one man in the museum, Jean-Marc Gentil, then its secretary-general, knew why he was there.

So far, Pei had not mentioned the project to anyone in the office. He had not even spoken to his partners about it. The only person in New York who knew of it was Eileen, with whom he talked about it at length. No foreign architect had ever left his mark on the Louvre, and Pei was still not at all certain that trying to do so was either possible or prudent.

Originally, Pei had been planning to make four visits to Paris, but after the third he was convinced that some sort of intervention was not only workable but necessary, and he decided that he would go forward. He then returned to Paris, meeting with Mitterrand and Lang. They made a formal offer of the job, and Pei agreed. 'I would not have accepted it if I hadn't studied the problem for months,' he said later. 'I concluded that it had to be done, and that I would be able to do it.'

In the course of the meeting, Pei explained in general terms his ideas about expansion, pointing out that the additional space required by the museum could be added by excavating the Cour Napoléon, the open area between the two wings built by Napoléon III. How the space was to be organised and entered was not then clear. Nevertheless, Mitterrand was encouraged. He seemed particularly impressed by Pei's sensitivity to the History of the Louvre as well as by the architect's determination nodded and said. 'Très bien.' For emphasis, he repeated it twice.

Back in New York, the project was treated with all the precautions due to a military secret. 'The idea of doing anything to the Louvre would have been killed if it had leaked out,' Pei said. A room was set aside on the eighth floor of Pei's offices, and although few of the rooms have locks on the doors, Pei made sure this one did – and that it was used. Soon after agreeing to take the job, Pei quietly contacted Yann Weymouth, who had worked with him in as a young designer on the East building before leaving to set up his own firm. Weymouth's mother was from Brittany, and he had lived for long periods in France and spoke the language fluently. In addition, felt Pei, Weymouth 'had the right spirit.' Weymouth agreed to rejoin the firm for the duration. Pei's son Didi, another architect on the East Building, was also assigned to the project, not least because he, too, spoke excellent French. Later, Pei picked yet another veteran of the East Building, Leonard Jacobson, to be the managing partner. Having given Jacobson only the bare outlines of the project, Pei finally telephoned him during a trip to Paris and asked him to phase himself out of his other assignments. 'I told him: The job is real. It's going to go; get yourself ready. I could feel the glee in his voice on the other end.'

Although Mitterrand and Biasini would both have qualified as the sort of powerful and interesting clients with whom Pei had traditionally done his best work, the Louvre itself became the true client for the project. Biasini said at one point that the Louvre 'occupies the subconscious' of France, and it came to occupy Pei's as well. Throughout the project, Pei and his French counterparts constantly la-boured in the shadow of the building's history; it was almost a tangible presence guiding their intentions.

At one point during a meeting held at the Pei office to discuss the re-distribution of works of art in the museum, Pei, Jacobson, and the Louvre's director, Michel Laclotte, were struggling with the fate of the museum's collection of paintings by Peter Paul Rubens. 'There are many ways of solving this problem architecturally,' said Pei, gesturing at the enormous roll of plans spread across the table. 'You must tell me how to do it from the museological point of view.' To which Laclotte replied, 'What is more important is whether the solution fulfils *l'esprit du Louvre*!' Pei and Jacobson both nodded. 'Of course, of course, *l'esprit du Louvre*!' they exclaimed almost simultaneously.

As Pei understood it, part of that spirit had to do with change. The building had undergone so many alterations and reincarnations over the centuries that he felt another chapter in the saga was perfectly appropriate to sustain the monument's vitality. And as he had done increasingly in recent years – especially in the East Building and with Freed at the Jarvits Center – he began to concentrate on how the Louvre was to be used, in this case, by even greater masses of people than it had accompanied before. 'Something had to be changed to involve the public,' he said.

The scope of that change appealed to him. Clearly, much more was at stake than mere architecture. Here was one of the greatest treasure houses of Western art and civilisation. Having studied not only the Louvre's history, but its position at the centre of Paris, Pei saw the challenge as one that also involved urban design, not to mention high-level trans-Atlantic diplomacy. As his thinking proceeded, Pei briefly discussed the project with his former client Richard Kahan. 'IM was approaching the problem like a real estate developer,' Kahan said. 'From the outset, he was planning the political strategy as well as the building.'

One of the fundamental early design issues was how to enter the reorganised museum. A superficial analysis might have suggested using the three existing entrances, one in each wing. That solution, Pei concluded, was not practical. The one in the northern wing was too small, another was cramped by historic staircases, and the third – on the Seine side – had already proved inadequate.

Denied those options, Pei concluded that logic all but demanded an entrance at the centre of the Cour Napoléon, where the museum's centre of gravity would eventually lie. An entrance in the corner of the court would, by bringing visitors equally close to all three wings, eliminate one of the Louvre's worst features, the need created by the main entrance on the Seine to walk long distances if the art one wanted to see was not in that wing. Few would mourn the loss of the courtyard, which had long ago become a parking lot for the finance ministry during the day and an unsavoury trysting place at night; in any case, it was not one of the Louvre's more distinguishing architectural spaces.

But having settled on a site for a new entrance, the question arose how it would be housed. Pei ruled out a freestanding masonry building, which would have obscured the facades of the embracing wings. He could go down into the spaces he had been planning from the start to excavate, but because the river was so close, he could not dig very deep, and simply decking over such a hole would produce an inhospitably shallow space for a proper entrance. 'I didn't want to create the effect of a subway station,' he explained. There had to be 'a room of importance, and there had to be light.'

The idea of a glass pyramid at the centre of the court emerged almost as much from Pei's study of classical French landscape design as it did from the need to get a roof high enough to avoid the subway station effect. Pei had read widely on the works of Le Nôtre, the greatest of French landscape architects, and was intrigued by the crisp geometry of his arrangements of plants, pathways, and water elements. One of Le Nôtre's common devices was to distribute plantings in a square pattern divided diagonally. Viewed from above, such a pattern resembled the floor plan of a pyramid. The pyramid form had much to recommend it. It was stylistically neutral and would therefore neither ape nor compete with the existing buildings. It was a basic geometric shape, which would blend with the classical symmetry of the Louvre and the gardens of the Tuileries to the west. And if it were clad in glass, it would, Pei hoped, be virtually transparent and intrude only minimally on the view of the existing architecture. It would also provide both the space for the 'room of importance' below and the light with which he wished to flood it. Pei predicted that the glazed surface would, as a bonus, reflect 'the changing moods of the Parisian skies.'

As Pei developed the idea, he extended subterranean passageways from the proposed underground space to each of the three wings of the Louvre. These would allow visitors to go directly to any of the museum's wings without making the traditional trek through galleries they had no interest in. He then added three smaller glass pyramids above the passageways both to bring in light and to allow visitors to orientate themselves as they moved from one wing to another. ('The measure of a large museum,' he said, 'is the clarity of its organisation.') Back on the surface, Pei flanked the main pyramid on three sides with reflecting pools that were pierced by fountains. The effect was to further lighten the form by making it appear to float on the water.

The rightness of the scheme seem equally compelling as architecture and as landscape architecture. Explaining it to a colleague in his New York office, Pei produced a copy of a book on Le Nôtre. Tapping the table with an almost boyish delight, he pointed to the elegantly ordered layout of one garden after another. 'Look at this!' he exclaimed. 'The love of geometry!'

The final design called for a main pyramid extending 116 feet on a side and raising to a peak of 71 feet, roughly two-thirds the height of the surrounding buildings. The three smaller pyramids were 26 feet on a side and 16 feet high, and the reflecting pools reached out into a 7.2-acre public plaza that was to be paved with granite. Reaching back through Fragrant Hill to the convictions that had allowed him to persuade Walter Gropius of the merits of his Shanghai art museum project, Pei declared, 'Architecture and landscape architecture cannot really be separated. In fact, some would say they are one and the same.' According to Michael Flynn, Pei's resident expert on curtain-wall construction, 'If IM Pei had had his druthers, he wouldn't have used any glass at all and just made a beautiful trellis. But unfortunately, you have to keep the rain out.'

When Pei had settled on the scheme to his satisfaction, he invited Biasini to New York for a visit. He had already prepared an elaborate wooden box model of the existing Louvre and had had four pyramids – one large and three small – made from polished Plexiglas. After Biasini had studied the wooden model, Pei, with full appreciation of the drama of the moment, produced the Plexiglas pyramids and positioned them in their proper places at the centre of

the model. 'Diamants! Diamants!' Biasin exclaimed. Then, switching to English, he declared, 'I like it! Let's go!'

For all the architect's insistence on the origins of the pyramid solution in Le Nôtre, it was vintage Pei. In fact, variations on the form had been with him since the early schemes for the Kennedy Library, which was to have included a truncated version. It had all the qualities that most appealed to the architect: it was geometrically pure, minimal, and sculptural. According to Theodore Musho, Pei's long-suffering collaborator on the Kennedy Library, the Louvre pyramid was for Pei 'a form waiting to get out.' Nevertheless, it had a special appropriateness in the new role Pei proposed for it. In addition to satisfying the practical requirements of the programme, it had direct links to the French Beaux-Arts tradition in its strict symmetry and unshakable rationality. (Despite his Harvard training under a Teutonic Modernist, Pei had never entirely lost touch with what he had learned at MIT, which was one of the last major American architecture schools to abandon the Beaux-Arts). And while there were obvious links to Egypt, they clearly had provided confirmation rather than inspiration for the design. As Pei pointed out, the Egyptian precedent was about mass and impenetrability, while his pyramid was about lightness and transparency. As for the proportions, which turned out to be the same as the Egyptians': 'We decided experimentally that they had been right 4,000 years ago. A few degrees steeper, and it's too aggressive; a few degrees less, and it seems to melt away.'

While the positioning of the pyramid at the centre of the Cour Napoléon may have satisfied the demands for symmetry imposed by the Louvre itself, it created a conflict in the larger Parisian scheme. The Louvre lies at the eastern end of the Voie Triomphale, the triumphal way that extends westward in a straight line through the Tuileries Gardens and the Place de la Concorde, up the Avenue des Champs-Elysées, and through the Arc de Triomphe. It is the most famous urban axis in the world. But the open arms of the Louvre wings are slightly off this grand axis, meaning that the pyramid, which Pei planned to position symmetrically in response to them, would seem askew when viewed from the west. (The problem had existed since the late 19th century, when the Tuileries Palace, which had terminated the axis from the west, was destroyed.)

This discontinuity had bedeviled many French architects, but having settled on the pyramid, Pei had virtually no choice about its relationship to the museum. The sense of order that dominates within the Cour Napoléon required that the new structure be aligned with the old. In any case, to align the pyramid with the grand axis would have to put a corner of the structure inside the Louvre's south wing and disrupted the organisation of the underground spaces on which the entire design was predicated. With a wry appreciation of the axil conundrum, Pei came up with a way to camouflage it. He proposed that a cast be made of an equestrian statue of Lous XIV by Bernini and that it be installed west of the pyramid. By aligning the statue with the triumphal way, Pei hoped that 'it would ameliorate an incoherent composition.'

Urban questions of another sort came into play when the project was looked at on its north-south axis. Because the passage through the Richelieu wing had long since been reserved for the finance ministry, there was no easy way for the public to get through that portion of the Louvre from the north or the south. This made it a major obstacle to the flow of pedestrians in the heart of the city during the day and virtually guaranteed that the Cour Napoléon would be

At the heart of Pei's plans for the pyramid was the hope that it would be nearly transparent. Here, the architect (wearing a hard hat bearing the Chinese character for his family name) demonstrates the clarity of the specially fabricated glass to President Mitterrand (left).

When no local firm could be found to fabricate critical parts for the complex 'bowstring' tensioning system that supported the glass, the architect turned to an American firm that specialised in rigging for racing yachts.

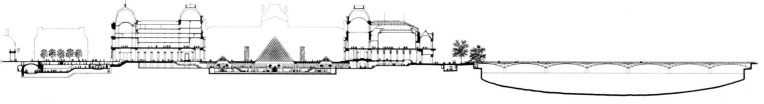

abandoned by all but the adventurous at night. By opening that passage, which lay across the Rue de Rivoli from the Palais-Royal subway station, Pei could not only provide an additional entrance to the museum (by dropping escalators into the underground corridor), but also ease the movement between the two banks of the Seine. (His main ally in this effort was Biasini, who fought so hard for it that the architects informally dubbed the space the 'passage Biasini.') Lighting the pyramid and its pools and fountain at night would, Pei was sure, reclaim the courtyard as an active urban space after hours. If this pyramid resonated with his classical schooling at MIT, his understanding of a museum renovation as an urban-planning opportunity could be traced directly to his practical experience with Zeckendorf.

While the public would come to focus on what Pei proposed above ground, the officials at the Louvre were most concerned with what was going to happen below the surface. This after all, was where the planning had begun, and what Pei proposed was no less Zeckendorfian in its ambitions than the 'tip of the iceberg', as the pyramid itself became known. The entire excavation was to provide for approximately 600,000 square feet on two levels. The focus was the space beneath the large pyramid. Here visitors would buy their tickets and be given information about the museum and where to find what they wished to see. From the central space, the three passages would lead them north, east, and south directly to the galleries, without the marathon journeys required by the existing layout. Another corridor would ultimately extend west, lit toward the end by a skylight in the form of an inverted pyramid and culminating in a vast underground terminal fed by a depressed roadway and intended to absorb the legions of tour buses that had for years clogged the nearby streets.

Surrounding the public spaces would be an auditorium, shops, and restaurants. And embracing all this would be two parallel tunnels served by electric carts and used for the transport of artworks (which formerly had to be winched in and out of gallery windows, weather permitting) and supplies for the other services. (Louvre officials insisted that the art and the food for the restaurants should not share the same tunnel.) One level below would be offices, laboratories for the maintenance and repair of works of art, and storage facilities. With total understatement, Weymouth described the complex as 'seven-acre basement with a fancy roof.' When complete, the added space would bring the Louvre's total area to more than two million square feet, making it the world's largest museum.

The scope of the Pei plan provided too much for the Louvre's director, André Chabaud, who resigned, saying that the reorganisation was 'unfeasible' and that 'architectural risks' lay ahead. Pei had no doubts. 'I sometimes have to pray hard that I'm correct,' he said. 'But this time, I was confident that we were on the right track.'

Mitterrand shared the architect's confidence, but urged Pei to move fast, because there were only five more years left of his seven-year term as president. 'It is a great pleasure,' Pei said, 'to work with someone who knows what he wants and will act on it.'

The atmosphere in the New York office when Pei returned from his meeting with the President was close to euphoric. Ian Bader, one of the younger architects assigned to the team, said Pei was convinced his design would be as well received by the French public as it had been by Mitterrand: 'IM was sure that everybody would join in his vision.'

As a formality, the proposal had to be presented to the Commission Supérieure des Monuments Historiques, an advisory group that had no binding authority, but carried considerable moral force in matters of Paris Landmarks. On January 23, 1984, Pei, Weymouth, Didi, and Biasini arrived for the presentation, which was held at the Ministry of Culture. But although the details of the project were supposed to have been kept secret, the architects could tell from mutterings as the room began to fill that things were not going to go their way. The lights were dimmed, and Didi, who was operating the slide projector, put up the first image. His father, who had been given a bamboo pointer that was so long he had to break off a piece to get it down to a comfortable size, began speaking with the help of a young woman who had been asked to translate. 'You could sense the hostility,' recalled Weymouth. 'It was palpable.'

Gradually the mutterings grew louder, until the 'delegates', including some reporters who had been alerted to the event and slipped in under cover, began attacking the design with abandon. The insults grew to such a pitch that the translator began to cry and she said she could not go on. A member of the audience volunteered to replace her, but the verbal assaults continued unabated. Finally, when the lights went up, three of the members of the committee rose to read prepared statements condemning a project they were supposed to be seeing for the first time. The committee's former chief architect, Bertrand Monnet, denounced it as something that was 'outside our mental space' and would prove to be a 'gigantic ruinous gadget.'

With the presentation in shambles, Biasini gathered up the Pei team and repaired to Chez Pauline, a classic Parisian bistro on the Rue Villedo, to assess the damage. Pei was less discouraged than angry at being treated unfairly. 'None of us had expected the vehemence of the opposition,' he said later. Weymouth suggested that they had been somewhat naïve and should have lobbied members of the committee before the meeting. With black humour, those present took bets on the margin of the committee's vote on the pyramid. (Didi, who predicted it would be unanimously negative, ultimately won.) Biasini, meanwhile put the best face on matters by saying that since Mitterrand was behind them, the opinion of the committee didn't necessarily matter.

The public didn't see it in that way. Parisians had become increasingly hostile to the incursions of modern architecture on their city. The dark hulk of the Montparnasse office tower that had gone up some years before on the southern edge of the city loomed as a reminder of the damage a single high-rise could do to the Paris skyline, and the faceless spires of the new office buildings of La Défense showed what could happen when such towers were assembled as a group. The latest attempt at low-rise Modernism, the tacky structures that had replaced the once-bustling markets of Les Halles, were scarcely better. In the light of such intrusions, it was perhaps predictable that almost anything new – especially in the bosom of the French cultural patrimony – would be received by the Parisians with scepticism at the least.

The Pei project was treated to much worse. Two days after the meeting of the historical monuments committee, a member of the French Academy, writing in *France-Soir*, predicted that the pyramid would be 'an atrocity' and accused Mitterrand of 'despotism.'[3] The only proper response, he declared, was 'insurrection.' *Le Quotidien de Paris* carried a piece warning that the design 'goes against the nature of the Louvre. It contradicts its biological development, its historic continuity.'[4] *Le Monde* headlined one story 'The House of the Dead' and compared Pei's

15

Because window-cleaning machinery would have been cumbersome if not hazardous to the sheer surface of the building, expert alpinists were hired to deal with the inevitable urban fallout.

Having won both his political and his architectural campaign, Mitterrand cuts the ribbon at the April 1989 opening of the pyramid.

Mitterrand and Pei tour the central space with culture minister Jack Lang.

proposal to 'an annex to Disneyland.'[5] Several critics insisted that a pyramid was by definition a closed form and that there was no aesthetically satisfactory way to put a door in it. A writer for *Le Figaro* condemned it as simply 'inadmissible.' Declared the paper, referring to Napoleon's campaign in Egypt, 'A new battle of the pyramids is about to begin.'[6]

A hasty poll taken by *Le Figaro* indicated that while 90 percent of its readers supported a renovation of the Louvre, only ten per cent supported the pyramid. A public petition was circulated asking, rhetorically, 'Will the Louvre be disfigured?' The fact that Mitterrand had dispensed with a competition in selecting an architect moved one prominent art historian to intone, 'It is unbecoming for a socialist president to act like a prince.' Many of the attacks combined French cultural chauvinism with a thinly veiled trace of xenophobia. 'I am surprised,' sniffed one opponent, 'that one would go looking for a Chinese architect in America to deal with the historic heart of the capital of France'. The art magazine *Connaissance des Arts*, which backed the pyramid from the start, received for its pains a stream of what approached racist mail. 'It was very unpleasant,' said the managing editor: 'There were letters saying the architect was neither French, nor even really American.'

While Biasini was confident that the president's blessing would be sufficient to carry the battle, he was enough of a veteran of French cultural clashes to realise that a counterattack was called for, and he proceeded to rally his troops. In a matter of days, he rounded up the Louvre's seven departmental curators and shuttled them and the design team to Arcachon, a small coastal resort west of Bordeaux, to frame a response. Once the group had assembled, Pei and his people put on a full-dress presentation, to which the curators – who were, after all, the people with the greatest artistic stake in the project – gave their unanimous support. Laclotte (who was then the Louvre's chief curator of paintings) insisted that the group produce a public statement of their views.

It was published on the last day of January and concluded 'In the context of the Grand Louvre, it seems to the Curators-in-Chief . . . that Mr. Pei's pyramid for the entrance to the museum, far from being (as has sometimes been said) a 'modernist gadget' or at best a 'gratuitous architectural gesture' is on the contrary an audacious concept that contributes to an architectural ensemble that for coherence and quality alike has been universally approved and accepted.[7]

The authority of the curator's statement did much to slow the momentum of the attacks, but it by no means halted them. Michel Guy, a former Minister of Culture, promptly founded the Association for the Renovation of the Louvre to mobilise resistance. He was less worried about the perceived threat posed by Pei's architecture than about the plan of reorganisation that underlay it. He favoured instead spending the money earmarked for the excavation and the pyramid on restoring the existing building and rearranging it into a loose conglomeration of 'mini-museums' that would concentrate on artistic themes and styles. Again invoking French cultural superiority, Guy told the Associated Press, 'I don't like the idea of everyone being treated like a tourist, that school-children or you or I should be obliged to follow the same trail as the Japanese who come only once.'[8] Even the American museum community eventually became alarmed, so much so that the French ambassador to Washington, Emmanuel de Margerie, had to call Pei in for a briefing to deal with the local protests. (Things

were not made easier by the fact that the project involved the removal from the Cour Napoléon of an equestrian statue of Lafayette that had been donated by the Daughters of the American Revolution.)

The debate went well beyond both architectural and museological issues. Some observers saw the opposition to the pyramid as a focus for the resentment felt by many on the political right for Mitterrand's socialist policies. As one French sociologist and historian, Jean-Paul Aron, described the situation, 'I see it as a manifestation of the hatred that the opposition holds for the left. For the left to take power in France has always been seen by the right as a monstrous possibility, as something that went against the laws of nature.'[9] Mitterrand's support was not strong all the time, and many expected him to lose control of the government in the parliamentary elections scheduled for 1986. Many of his harshest critics suspected him of trying with the pyramid to enshrine his administration before he left office.

The ideological crisis over the Louvre engendered a behind-the-scenes struggle at the highest levels of the Parisian world of art and society. Pierre Boulez, the renowned orchestra conductor, played a vigorous role lobbying his friends in favour of the pyramid. One of those friends was Claude Pompidou, the widow of the former conservative president. Madame Pompidou was arguably the most powerful woman in France and was widely considered its unofficial cultural ambassador. Despite the fact that her husband had been on the political right, he had broken with tradition in commissioning the controversial Pompidou Centre, and his widow was now willing to put her own influence behind the pyramid. In a magazine interview, she declared (with an impression about authorship that would have wounded Henry Cobb), 'I am convinced that Pei's pyramid will be very beautiful. I have seen a magnificent tower he built in Boston, and a project for the bank of China in Hong Kong; truly one can have confidence in this architect!'[10] One of her friends went so far as to say, 'It was a Mitterrand project, but there is no doubt that her support clinched it.'

Happily for the Pei forces, Madame Pompidou was regarded with special affection by Jacques Chirac, the the mayor of Paris and the president of one of the two leading opposition political parties. It would have been politically correct for Chirac to condemn the pyramid, but following a discreet meeting with Pei himself, he announced that he was 'not hostile' to the project. However, he did ask Pei to have a full-scale mock-up of the pyramid erected on the site so that the public could get a more accurate ideas of the impact it would have on its surroundings. This overtly populist gesture was seen by the architects as particularly important because, as Weymouth explained the situation later, 'We didn't have one client we had 55 million clients, the entire population of France!'

In the Spring of 1985, a crane was moved to the position in the Cour Napoléon where the pyramid was to stand, and from its extended arm four cables were stretched outward to simulate the ridges of the pyramid. Because the glass of the real pyramid's walls was to be clear, the architects explained, the outlines alone provided an accurate impression of what the building would look like when finished. They were well aware that the finished building would be only partially transparent, but if the truth about that was shaded for the public consumption, the cables did not convey a fair idea of the size of the structure, which many people were surprised to see was not as large as they had feared. The cables were left in place for four days, during which time an estimated 60,000 Parisians trooped by for a look. Almost overnight, the tide of public opinion began to turn. *Le Figaro* and several other newspapers that opposed the pyramid suddenly fell silent on the issue.

But the debate continued to rage elsewhere. The American architecture critic Charles Jencks, a vociferous supporter of the Post-Modern movement, mounted an especially sharp attack in the September 1985 issue of the British magazine *Art & Design*, declaring that Pei had succumbed to 'megalomania.' Jencks, who felt Pei had redeemed himself for his earlier Modernist 'malaprops' with Fragrant Hill, accused him of backsliding in Paris: 'It is well known that Boulée and Le Corbusier suffered from this, occasionally: for Hitler and [his architect, Albert] Speer the disease was chronic. It is also known that the ego is most likely to be infected near the centre of great cities, such as Paris, so when Mr Pei went to talk to Mr Mitterrand about adding a few new entrances to the Louvre one could guess the dreaded disease might strike again . . . Now Pei and Mitterrand have succumbed to the same virus, and for much the same reason: they want a memorial to their memory which one cannot avoid.'[11]

Having rested the momentum from the French anti-pyramid forces, Pei's supporters were dispirited to see the English-speaking press take up the attack. Nevertheless, Pei responded with characteristic determination. According to Ian Bader, who worked closely with him at the New York end during the entire period, the pressure in the office was 'mind-boggling, shells were landing all over, but IM never showed it for a moment.'

Even though the French public seemed to be coming around, the possibility that Mitterrand might be crippled politically in the next elections cast a lingering shadow over the project. Conceivably, the work already done might still be shelved. Jean Lebrat, the buoyant French *fonctionnaire* who had been put in charge of the construction phase of the project, urged all parties to speed things up so that it would be 'irréversible.' By the end of April 1986, the central excavations in the Cour Napoléon had been finished. There was no turning back.

Picking up the pace proved to have been a wise precaution, for in short order, politics again intervened to threaten the plan. In the parliamentary elections, Mitterrand's socialists suffered precisely the reverses Pei and his people had feared, losing power to a conservative coalition led by Chirac, who became prime minister, leaving the president to share power with a right-wing government. Although Chirac had earlier declared himself 'not hostile' to the pyramid, Edouard Balladur, his finance minister, was not so sympathetic. From the very beginning, the plan had been to remove the finance ministry from the Richelieu wing. Pei had said often that he would probably not have accepted the Louvre commission if the ministry was going to remain in place. New accommodations for the ministry were already under construction on the banks of the Seine in Bercy, a section of eastern Paris that had been until recently the centre of the wine trade. The main finance offices had already been vacated by the former finance minister, Pierre Bérégovoy, who transferred his people to temporary quarters on the Boulevard Saint-Germain on the Left Bank, and were in the process of demolition. (Bérégovoy, a supporter of the pyramid, had gone so far as to make sure that a hole was put in his roof before he left to encourage further demolition.)

But Balladur, a little-loved civil servant who served as

Chirac's second-in-command, after nearly three months in office decided that he didn't want to be so far away from the centre of the city – and power. After all, the ministry had been in the Louvre since 1873, having moved after its own building was destroyed by fire during the Commune. Its accommodations on the Rue de Rivoli included high-ceilinged offices furnished with red velvet chairs and embellished with gilded moldings, crystal chandeliers, and marble fireplaces. Quite apart from the loss of such luxury, the move would break what the Parisians call the 'sacred triangle,' the link between the Elysée Palace, home to French presidents since 1873, the Hotel Matignon, the prime minister's headquarters since 1958, and the Louvre. So on July 29, 1987, Balladur announced that his civil servants would remain in the Louvre until 'appropriate space can be found for them in the centre of Paris,' a process expected to take as long as ten years. He then ordered the Richelieu offices restored (at a cost of some 20 million dollars) and moved his senior people back into the Louvre. Without the Richelieu wing, of course, the entire rationale for the pyramid would be compromised, since the wing was to account for most of the 82 percent overall gain of exhibition space. Many saw Balladur's move as an insidious attempt to derail the entire project.

Yet again, Pei refused to buckle, or even to complain openly. 'I was very sad at that moment,' he said, 'but the logic of the plan was so strong that I was sure it would prevail.'

In fact, Balladur's high-handed manner did little to help his own cause, and the press took to needling him for such imperial gestures as having white-gloved footmen in his dining room and decorating his office with antiques from the museum's collection. Chirac at this point had his eye on the presidency, but his chances were fading as Mitterrand rebounded at the polls. Meanwhile, Balladur's stand against the Louvre expansion was costing him support among his own colleagues in the cabinet. In January of 1988, having been advised to face the increasingly likely prospect of a conservative defeat in the may presidential elections, Balladur finally agreed (after a quiet lunch with Pei and the Minister of Culture) to have half of his people out by the end of the year.

By this time, Biasini had reached the mandatory retirement age of 65 and was succeeded by Pierre-Yves Ligen, who had worked with Biasini in the Ministry of Culture under Malraux and had been director of urban planning for Paris under Chirac when he was still mayor. Meanwhile Michel Laclotte, the curator of paintings who had played such an important role in framing the Arcachon statement, had been named by Mitterrand to be director of the Louvre. In the past, the post had been held by administrators rather than art historians and had always been subservient to the division of the Ministry of Culture that oversaw all national museums. But the job was now redefined to give Laclotte an authority comparable to that of Carter Brown at the National Gallery. Laclotte found Pei somewhat 'obstinate' but conceded that 'all great artists are like that' and put his new power behind the pyramid, which was no longer a mere cable mock-up, but a fully glazed presence gleaming beneath a film of construction dust outside Balladur's windows. At a 'soft' opening on March 4, arranged with an eye to the elections that were only two months away, Mitterrand conferred on Pei the Légion d'Honneur – and made a conspicuous point of holding the ceremony inside the pyramid.

In May, Mitterrand prevailed at the polls, forcing Chirac

For the first time in centuries the intact walls of the original castle have brought to light the crypt of the Cour Carrée.

Although Pei's renovation of the Cour Napoléon is no less abstract than the design for the pyramid itself, the space is far more inviting than many of the architect's previous plazas.

If the pyramid is less transparent during the day than Pei had hoped, it becomes a see-through jewel when lit at night. Its position slightly off the axis of the Champs-Elysées is wryly mitigated by the addition of a cast of Bernini's statue of Louis XIV to anchor the line of site.

Pei with the cable mock-up that was intended to show the public what it could expect when the pyramid was finished. Although somewhat deceptive, the exercise proved convincing and turned the tide of criticism.

and Balladur to resign. Bérégovoy again became finance minister and promptly turned to packing his people's bags for Bercy. Almost two years had been lost in combating Balladur's rearguard action. Pei, who had never doubted that time would bring him victory, joked that 'the Chinese invented bureaucracy, but the French perfected it.'

Two months after the elections, Pierre Boulez conducted a concert at the pyramid for the benefit of le tout Paris, who by their well-heeled presence gave the project an indelible social imprimatur and hardly seemed to mind that the second half of the performance was rained out. Said Pei, flanked by Eileen and Didi and grinning widely beneath his umbrella, 'I've been waiting a long time for this.' (It wasn't quite long enough for Leonard Jacobson, who had been instructed to have the reflecting pools filled and the fountains playing for the occasion, whatever the costs. The machinery later had to be drained and disassembled so that it could be fine-tuned. 'I was purple,' Jacobson later confessed.)

On October 14, 1988, Mitterrand cut a tricoloured ribbon leading to the Cour Napoléon, officially opening the courtyard to the public, and thousands of Parisians streamed in for their first close-up look. The following March 30, at 4:30 on an unseasonably hot afternoon, the president cut yet another ribbon, this one to mark the opening of the 'room of importance' beneath the pyramid.

What the first unofficial visitors to penetrate the interior saw was a spectacle of engineering as well as design. Pei and his people had created an almost sublimely simple object with the most sophisticated of means – and occasionally against what seemed to be insurmountable technological odds.

Acquiring the right glass was a saga in itself. Pei had insisted from the outset that it be absolutely clear in order to make the pyramid as nearly transparent as possible. Virtually all the glass available on the market, however, was made with small amounts of iron oxide, which gave it a slightly greenish tint. In hopes of finding something more suitable, the Pei team approached the centuries-old French firm of Saint-Gobain, the country's biggest glass manufacturer. Pei's people were told that Saint-Gobain, too, had abandoned the technique for making totally clear glass years ago. What they wanted was simply 'impossible.' That answer was not good enough for Michael Flynn, who had handled the design for the skylight at the East Building. He tracked down a German firm which, while it had not done such a thing in recent memory, said it would be willing to resuscitate the craft for such a prestigious use. Flynn took the Germans' information back to the people at Saint-Gobain, who quickly appreciated the threat to French manufacturing pride. After extensive consultations, the firm concluded that it could, after all, produce the material Pei wanted by using a pure white sand from a quarry in Fontainbleau. 'They came around when they realised how deadly in earnest we were,' noted Flynn. As it turned out, the German product would have cost less, but buying French prevailed.

A similar exchange ensued over the subject of polishing the glass. If treated in the normal way, the sheets required for the pyramid would show minor variations in their surface. This would be invisible under ordinary circumstances, and even the slightest imperfections would compromise the crystalline effect for which Pei was striving. In this case, the French were not able to provide the service and agreed to have their glass shipped to an English factory that could.

The 675 diamond-shaped and 118 triangular panes that were eventually installed were held together by a structural system that involved some major innovations on the designers' part. Again to minimise any obstructions to the view through the pyramid, Pei called for a solution that made the spaceframes in the Kennedy Library and the Jarvits Center seem almost clumsy. 'There were 12 ways to do it, but IM Pei pushed for a large number of small structural members,' said Jacobson, who was responsible for making the whole thing work. The result was a steel spiderweb made up of 128 crisscrossing girders secured by 16 thin cables. Unable to find any European sources for nodes and struts of sufficient strength and lightness for this 'bowstring' tensioning system, Pei turned to Navtec, a maker of rigging for America's Cup Yachts, in Littleton, Massachusetts. (One of the few low-tech solutions for the problems posed by the pyramid was the one used for cleaning the glass. Because the exterior surface was so pristine, and the interior surface so difficult to reach through the spiderweb, the designers hired a team of trained moutaineers who were able to negotiate the structure without damaging it.)

Since the political uncertainties made it necessary to get the pyramid itself up faster than they would have liked, the members of the construction team were also faced with the problem of how to support the metal frame while the work that normally would have preceded it continued below ground. The problem was solved by erecting concrete columns from the foundations up to ground level at an early stage of the excavation. They were later connected by 150-ton box girders that were bowed upwards in anticipation of their ultimate load by cables attached to the ends. The cables were gradually loosened as work on the pyramid progressed, until, when the superstructure was finished, the girders were allowed to return to the horizontal. So accurate were the advance calculations for the process that not a single pane of glass in the pyramid broke when the last cable was released.

For all its technological complexity, the pyramid itself was, of course, only a relatively small part of the total undertaking. The combined area of the underground construction was larger than the entire floor space of the East Building. In the course of excavating for it, the architects came upon an additional opportunity. Just below the surface of the Cour Carrée – the enclosed courtyard to the east of the Cour Napoléon – were found the remains of an earlier Louvre. They were the 12th-century foundations of the fortress erected by Philippe Auguste and portions of the palace of Charles V. Archeologists had long known they were there, but were surprised to find them in such good condition and proposed that they be restored. A crew of 58 specialists promptly went to work, and their discoveries ultimately led to the largest archaeological operation ever carried out in France. Altogether in the Cour Carrée and the Cour Napoléon, some 25,000 historic objects were found, ranging from ceramic shards and a cooking pot with pigeon bones still in it to a ceremonial helmet thought to have been stolen from the palace and abandoned by the thief. Plans were immediately made to link the foundations to the Pei design as a separate exhibition area, using the covered moat of the original fortress as a subterranean passageway.

With that behind them, the architects returned to work on the new construction. The floor plan of Pei's main space, christened the Hall Napoléon, shows a large square rotated beneath the square of the pyramid to form what appears

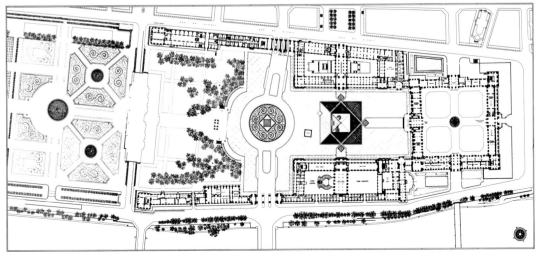

Pei had hoped to install the Winged Victory *atop the column supporting the entrance platform, but the Louvre officialdom felt the public outcry over moving it would be too great and left it where it was.*

from above to be an eight-pointed star. Its walls and floor were faced in a creamy limestone quarried at Chassagne in the Burgundy wine country and similar in colour to that of the facades of the old building. To give the concrete of the coffered ceiling a comparably warm tone, special sand was brought in from the Nièvre valley and added to the mixture. The attention paid to the finish of the concrete exceeded even that in the East Building; ironworkers who were installing reinforcing elements were obliged to wear slippers so that the wooden forms would not be marred by their boots. The goal, said Pei, was to make it appear as if the underground space had been 'carved out of a single block of stone.'

Protecting this extraordinary labyrinth from the elements was another formidable challenge. When the Seine floods, water can rise to within a few feet of the surface of the ground, so a drainage network was designed capable of pumping out even the worst floods. To satisfy French fire regulations, 26 fire exits were threaded to the perimeter of the Cour Napoléon, where they were covered with three-ton cast iron grilles designed to open automatically in an emergency.

Pei had always involved himself in many of the minor details as well as the major decisions of buildings under his direct responsibility. For the Louvre, he was even more attentive than usual. The helicoidal staircase leading from the entrance platform to the floor of the main space is a typical example. Pei was eager that the metal supports for the stone steps be as thin as possible at the outside edges. But his advisers told him that a minimum thickness was required to keep the steps from bouncing under the anticipated traffic. Pei promptly trimmed back the steel to get the visual effect he was seeking, but then increased the weight of the stone treads to dampen any vibration of the steel. Both aesthetics and engineering were perfectly served. According to a French specialist working on the project, 'We were always doing the impossible to cope with the architectural design. People have never seen anything so closely detailed.'

Jean Lebrat, who had overseen the construction of the Les Halles complex, among other major Paris projects, was particularly impressed by what he called the 'inevitability' of Pei's architecture. As he put it, 'The rigour of the geometry ruled out souplesse – there was no chance for multiplicity of solutions. With other architects, one changes the design to correct for what is possible, to accommodate the unbuildable elements of the design. But with Pei, it had been so well thought out that we could not build any other way. He has a complete vision, which he lets others discover on their own. It took me a long time to understand that. It was diabolique!'

Even though the project as a whole had been made *irréversible*, Mitterrand maintained an intense personal interest in its progress. On several occasions, he would slip away from the Elysée at night and, accompanied by Pei and a few bodyguards, inspect the site in secret. On one of the visits, Pei saw Mitterrand bend over and almost reverently touch the water from one of the reflecting pools as it glided in a perfect, thin sheet over one of the granite weirs.

By the time the Hall opened to the public, the agonies of the early days had been all but forgotten. For those determined to keep up the attack, the thrust shifted from the pyramid to the reorganisation of the collections and the prospect of making the museum too popular. (To which the prickly Laclotte, sounding very much like Carter Brown at the National Gallery, was quick to reply, 'This is the way we

experience art today, en masse, and architecture must accommodate it.')

Some of the newspapers that had devoted so much space to condemning the Pei design now found that it wasn't so bad after all. Conceded a writer in *Le Quotidien de Paris*, 'The much-feared pyramid has become adorable.'[12]

A few observers with a taste for history noted wryly how the flip-flop in official opinion resembled the one a century before over the Eiffel Tower. In 1887, *Le Monde* had run an article representing the views of some 300 French writers and artists protesting, 'in the name of art and the threatened history of France,' the plans to build 'the useless and monstrous Eiffel tower.' The artists insisted that the construction would 'crush with its barbaric, factory-chimney weight' the 'pristine beauty of Paris.' No less a figure than Emile Zola condemned it as 'a pile of iron junk.'[13] The original supporters of the pyramid took special delight in the turn of the historic wheel, pointing to a Louis Harris poll taken after the opening that showed 56 percent of those surveyed in favour of the pyramid, with only 23 against, an almost exact reversal of the numbers four years before.

Congratulations poured in from around the world. *Le Figaro*, one of Pei's sharpest early critics, hastily reserved the pyramid to celebrate the tenth anniversary of its magazine supplement. (Amazed at the paper's cheeky loss of memory, Biasini asked Mitterrand if he didn't also think it a bit much. The president replied that he considered it 'droll.') Dignitaries lined up for escorted tours. Among them was Britain's Prince Charles, who had made a name for himself as an amateur architecture critic by attacking most of the recent modern buildings in London. With unexpected enthusiasm, he pronounced Pei's work 'marvellous, very exciting.'

The building was not without its problems. The main one was that, for all the efforts to make the pyramid an intangible crystalline presence, it was sufficiently opaque under some weather conditions to disappoint even the architect. (And no one had quite anticipated the amount of dirt that would accumulate on it in a short time, despite the best efforts of the alpinists.) The air conditioning proved inadequate on a hot day, and the escalators were balky. Some visitors found the acoustics of the mainspace excessively harsh. And the public excitement over the building produced such crowds that long lines formed at the main entrance despit Pei's planning for increased capacity.

One shortcoming that was as much a disappointment to Pei as it was to visitors who knew about it was the absence of a piece of sculpture atop the concrete column that rose in the centre of the Hall Napoléon to support the reception platform inside the front door. From the beginning of the plan, Pei had hoped fervently that he would be able to secure the *Winged Victory of Samothrace* for this proud spot. Indeed, it appeared in all the early drawings. But its position at the top of a famous flight of stairs in the old building was so much a part of the Louvre's traditions that even Laclotte decided he could not risk the reaction to moving it. Several other candidates were considered and rejected. A replica of Rodin's *Thinker* was another possibility, but the anatomy didn't lend itself to a view from below. Another was a cast of an abstract rooster by Brancusi, who had died leaving only the plaster version. (Disputes over casting it put an end to that idea.) For an architect who had made such enthusiastic use of sculpture as a counterpoint to his work (and who had won virtually every other gamble on this project), the failure to secure the Samothrace for the pyramid was particularly painful.

There was much else for the Pei people yet to do. In a future phase of the project, the entire Richelieu wing would have to be rebuilt on the inside to transform it from offices to galleries. Landscaping of the gardens west of the pyramid, including the installation of a 'ghost' outline of the foundations of the vanished Tuileries palace, would take months. So would the cleaning of the museum's limestone facades. The completion of the underground parking facility was years off.

Yet the structure that opened in the Spring of 1989 was in every way at the heart of Pei's work. His fundamental love of geometric precision had found precisely the right setting. So had his feeling for landscape and the relationship of a building to the life of a city. His Modernist rigour had rehabilitated a Neo-Classical monument through a form that resonated with history reaching back 800 years – or 4,000, if the Egyptian precedent is included – and yet pushed at the limits of contemporary technology.

And it worked for those that used it. As he had in the East Building and at Fragrant Hill, Pei exploited the movement of people through his volumes as a way to animate the crisp joints and satin finishes of his forms. Eerily correct as the uninhabited Cour Napoléon looked with its glass centre-piece and equally glassy pools, it required pedestrians to make the space complete. Shortly before the courtyard opened, Weymouth, who had worked with Pei to find just the right stone for the spherical bollards on the edge of the space, noticed a young couple taking in the view with their child. Suddenly, the little girl walked up to one of the grey balls, studied it for a moment, then wrapped her arms around it and kissed it. 'I broke into tears,' said Weymouth. 'We had worked for that for six years.'

Here, Pei had found the equation that had been missing in the plaza of the Dallas City Hall and others of his overly abstract public spaces. The day before the opening, the architect was spotted across the street that penetrates both wings of the Louvre at the western edge of the Cour Napoléon, surveying the crowds surging around the new

building. He had been there tor some minutes, unrecognised by all but a few of the visitors. When an acquaintance joined him on the narrow strip of curb left by a construction fence, Pei told him that he had just seen a dog leap into one of the reflecting pools for a swim. 'It's so festive,' the architect said to his surprised listener. 'I didn't mind at all.'

The profit gained from the contrast between inanimate forms and human activity proved even more effective inside. Indeed, the helicoidal staircase with its lighted treads – which took its spiral forebear in the Everson Museum to unthought-of levels – verged on the theatrical, especially with the freestanding, piston-like elevator in its centre. And by creating such startling views of the old buildings through the glass from below, Pei overcame the traditionally negative associations of being underground and actually amplified the appreciation of what had gone before. The old Louvre was no longer just an aged enclosure, but an active element in a redefined architectural composition.

Shortly before the gala dinner celebrating the opening, Pei was seen bustling around the hall giving last-minute instructions to museum employees in their new Yves Saint-Laurent uniforms on the arrangement of the planters for the ornamental trees. It was the same ritual he had performed hours before the opening of Fragrant Hill, but here it was not to conceal shoddy workmanship. It was to perfect the experience for his guests, who included much of the transatlantic cultural élite and most of his family, who had come both for the opening and for Didi's wedding the next day. Halfway through the dinner itself, Jack Lang rose to toast 'notre ami, Pei.' The architect was then ushered to the microphone and said a few words in his heavily accented French. He paused, evidently searching his vocabulary, and then, in a voice that betrayed a rare tremor, added. 'Merci pour tout.'

Reflecting on the occasion some weeks later, Pei said. 'I hope to do many more things, but never again will I have another opportunity like the Louvre.'

This feature is based on an extract from the book The Architecture of I M Pei *by Carter Wiseman, published by Abrams in USA and by Thames & Hudson in UK, and is reproduced here by kind permisson of the publishers.*

Notes

1 The incident is described by Ronald Koven in 'Pei's Paris Pyramid,' *Boston Globe*, August 7, 1988.

2 Quoted by Mark Stevens, 'Pyramid Scheme,' *Vanity Fair*, June 1988, p 52.

3 Jean Dutord, 'Appel à l'insurrection,' *France-Soir*, January 26, 1984.

4 Bruno Foucart, 'Le Grand Louvre et sa pyramide,' *Le Quotidien de Paris*, January 26, 1984.

5 André Fermigier, 'La maison des morts,' *Le Monde*, January 26, 1984.

6 Henry Bernard, 'Un gadget inutile,' *Le Figaro*, January 28, 1984.

7 The statement was widely reported; the full text was published in *Le Monde*, February 3, 1984.

8 Quoted by Mary Blume in 'It's Adieu to the Dingy, Difficult Louvre,' *International Herald Tribune*, February 2, 1989.

9 Quoted by Richard Bernstein in 'I M Pei's Pyramid,' *New York Times Magazine*, November 24, 1985.

10 Claude Pompidou in an interview with Philippe de l'Estang, *Galeries*, May 1985.

11 Charles Jencks, 'Symbolism and Blasphemesis,' *Art & Design*, September 1985, p 42.

12 Bruno Foucart in *Le Quotidien de Paris*, March 30, 1989.

13 Quoted by Edward Cody in 'Louvre Pyramid Makes a Glowing Debut,' *International Herald Tribune*, July 5, 1988.

GÜNTER BEHNISCH
THE GERMAN POSTAL MUSEUM, FRANKFURT

The German Postal Museum by Günter Behnisch is the third such institution in Frankfurt, having been preceded by the Imperial and Federal Museums before it. Due to the convenient location of the Imperial Museum, and the public preoccupation with technological progress at the time, this museum was a great success, with attendance figures that were impressive even by today's standards. Following the war, the collection was stored in various warehouses in and around Frankfurt, and a portion of it was exhibited in a villa on the Schaumainkai that was designated as the Federal Postal Museum in 1956. While there was some initial enthusiasm for a strategy of integrating the dissipated collection with that of a new postal museum in Bonn, the idea was abandoned when the Frankfurt city council announced its plans for a 'Museumsufer' or riverside promenade of museums along the Schaumainkai. Günter Behnisch and Partners were the subsequent winners of a competition for the new headquarters of the collection, which was to be brought together and updated for the first time in 50 years.

The decision to locate this facility on the same site as the villa that had served as the Federal Postal Museum had the advantage of providing both symbolic and physical continuity, but the restricted size of the plot made planning of an annex very difficult. Provision for any future expansion, which experience has shown to be a necessary requirement in museum design, was also a potential problem, due to the lack of space. In addition, the old mansion was in great need of restoration if it was to retain any active role in the new institution. As Thomas Werner, the Director of the new museum has said, the architect's idea of placing a portion of the exhibition area underground has meant that: 'The plant-covered roof of the main exhibition floor takes up the character of the old garden, and the clear division of the old and new building parts towards the outside avoided the problems usually arising when old and new buildings are linked directly with one another. A truncated glass cone at the back of the garden connects the different storeys of the new building in a kind of patio and provides the inside of the building with a unique transparency, at the same time allowing daylight to fall into the underground exhibition floor. The motif of the semicircle is repeated in some other parts of the building such as where the building was constructed around the root bales of the existing trees. These semicircular elements are intended to form a contrast to the otherwise linear new building.'

The German Postal Museum has five floors, of which two are underground. The first of these is used as the main exhibition floor, and the architect has established a connection between it and a corresponding level in the existing villa, which has not only expanded the available exhibition space, but has also ensured that the older building will continue to be utilised. The second underground level is used as a car-park, once again to maximise space usage, as well as providing much needed storage space.

The entire ground floor, which has been liberated by this design strategy, has been turned over to entrance requirements with an information desk, museum shop, cafeteria and auditorium located here. Two upper levels are reserved for permanent and temporary exhibitions respectively, with security of temporary displays of postage stamps being an important factor in the location and design of that area. An amateur radio station has been installed on the roof, continuing the Museum's commitment to technological implementation and display. The attitude taken towards exhibitions has been best summed up by the Museum Director:

'The concept of the exhibition was designed by a group of experts from the various branches of the Deutsche Bundespost on the basis of a design drawn up by the Düsseldorf Institute for Social Psychology. The result is a museum which not only intends to impart the technical aspects of postal and telecommunications history to visitors but which regards the history of communications as an integral part of the development of individuals, societies and nations.'

The architect has intentionally set out to contrast the new building with the old, in terms of materials and space planning; believing that this has allowed much more design freedom and is more in keeping with the forward looking, technologically-based image that the Deutsche Bundespost seeks to convey. Such contrast has also allowed a more decentralised organisation of exhibitions, using the open, three-dimensional spaces that have resulted to best advantage.

Great care was taken to save as many trees as possible on the site, which has provided a park-like setting for the museum. Achieving this was not easy, because construction of underground parking and exhibition areas required special replanting techniques. Fortunately, this task was made more straight-forward as many of the largest trees were located near the edge of the property.

Rather than responding to fixed exhibition requirements, Günter Behnisch has provided an architectural solution that encourages flexibility and change. As he has said, 'It is our experience that achievement in art is greater and ultimately better and more varied if relatively difficult problems have had to be overcome . . . and the creation of an exhibition is probably no different.' The freshness of his own approach to the seemingly impossible quandaries presented in this particular case have provided additional support for this theory.   *JS*

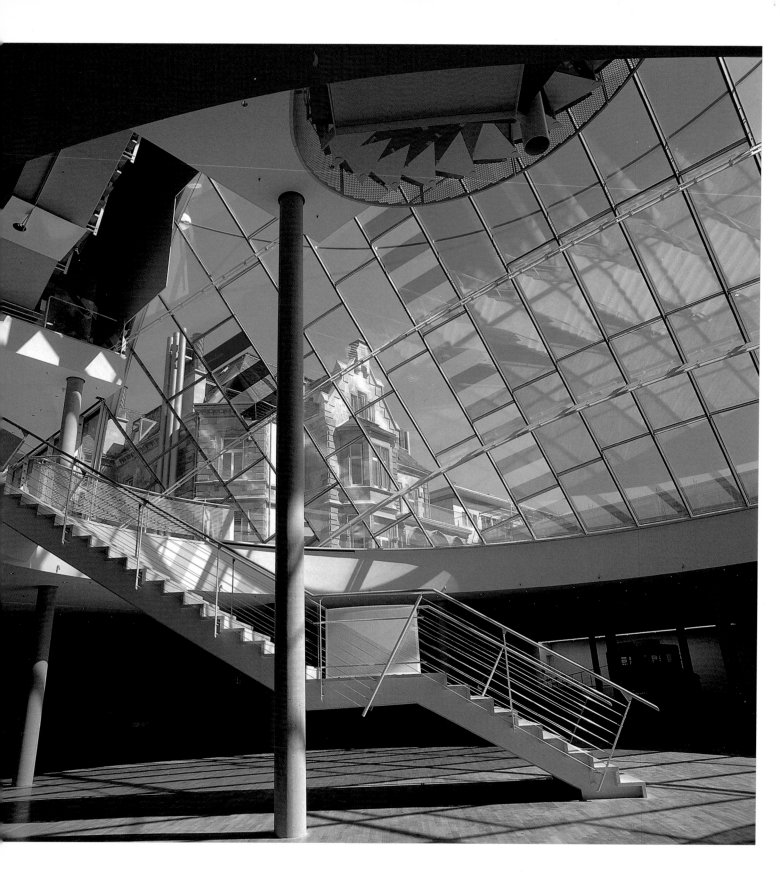

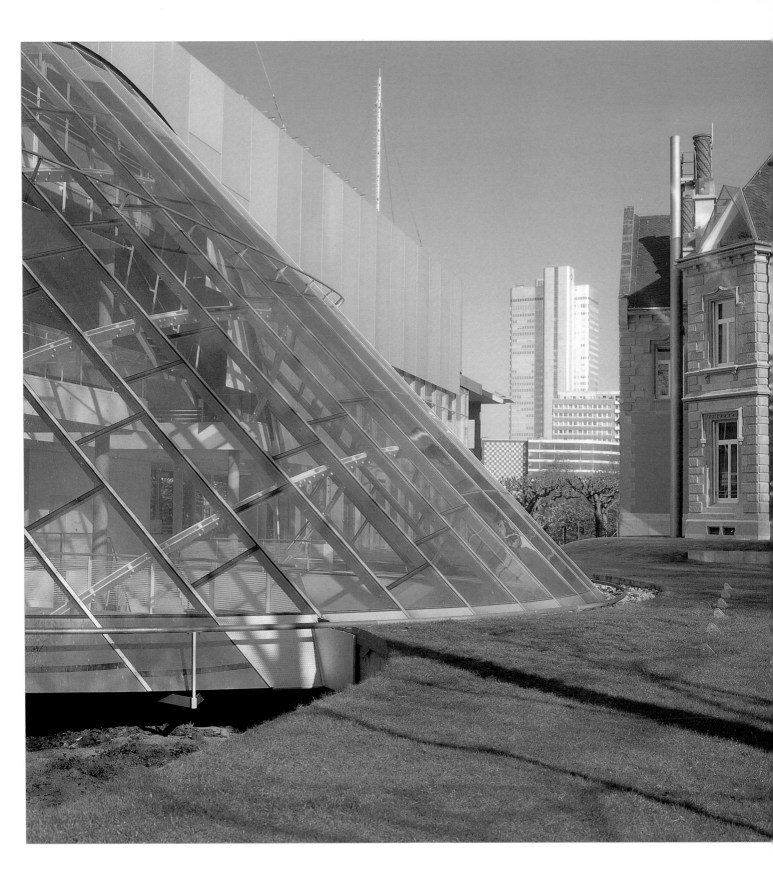

TADAO ANDO
I HOUSE

The house is situated amongst pine trees on the banks of the River Ashiya which flows between Osaka and Kobe. It is in an exclusive, residential district and has a view of the sea.

I house, which also includes guest rooms, is for an elderly couple, their son and his wife. Designed to provide both couples and any guest with privacy, the two households are independent, although the building allows the members to lead interlocking lives.

The composition is centred around a cylindrical volume with a radius of 7.44 m, enclosing a multi-storey space. The topmost floor, a 6.5 m x 29.1 m cuboid, is capped by a vault that is a sixth of a circle in section.

The cylinder is situated in the western part of the house's location, the entire building having an L-shaped plan. The rest of the site is given over to a sloping, walled-in garden and it is on to this that the three-storey space within the cylinder opens.

The three floors of the building are connected by the multi-storey cylinder. From the first-floor entrance hall, one can go either to the lower storey or to the second floor. The central facilities of the house are located in the basement. These include: the dining-room, kitchen, living-room, tatami-room, and bedroom for the parents. The guest rooms and hall are on the first floor. The bedroom and living-room for the son and his wife are on the second floor. Every room has a view of the garden which becomes blanketed in white in the spring when flowers bloom. In this way, the passing seasons allow for variety to the landscape.

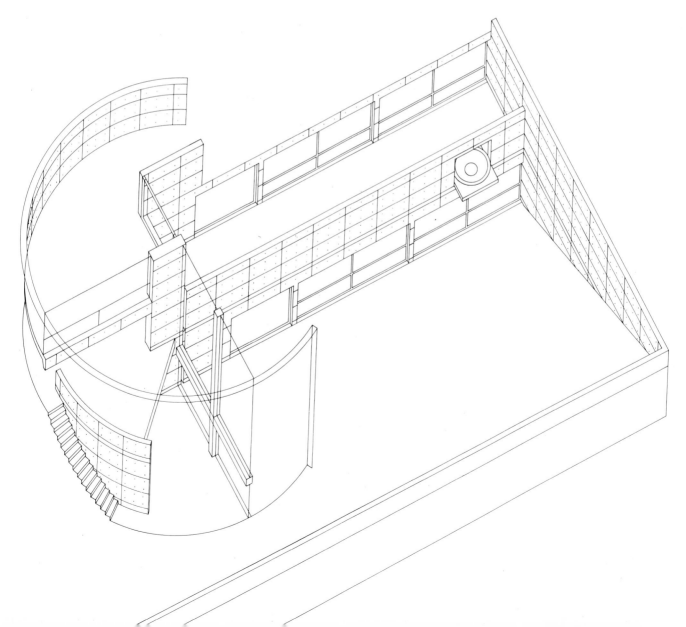

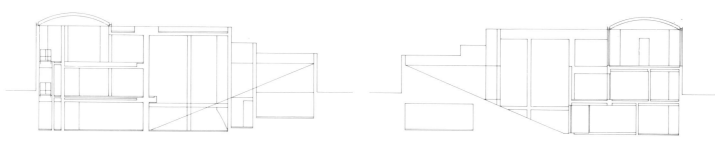

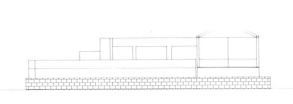

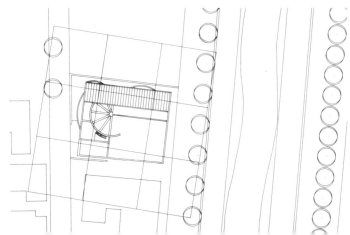

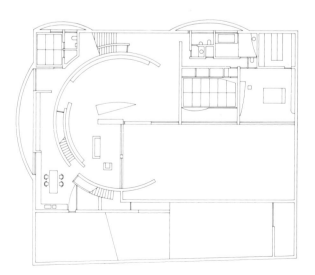

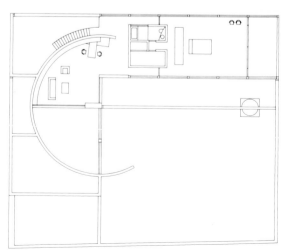

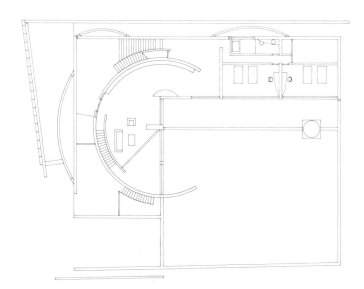
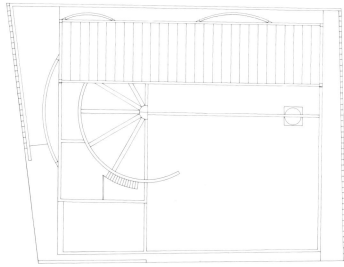

PHILIPPE STARCK
RECENT PROJECTS

LAGUIOLE KNIFE FACTORY, FRANCE
Jean-Louis Costes, of the Café Costes, loves his country, architecture and me.

As for myself, I love him too.

This is why I accepted with pleasure when he asked me to build, with subsidies from the town hall, a factory for these knives which are so symbolic of the heart of our beloved France.

The factory, situated amongst magnificent mountains, had to be economical, use local potential and above all have a very strong image.

I am not interested in the idea that architecture has no need of charity in order to survive and open out, if it can become, in a noble way, an accomplice to industry and commerce.

Architecture can help the renowned and the propagation of the renowned.

By rendering this service, it no longer even has the need of a cultural pretext to find the necessary subsidies for its accomplishment. The Laguiole factory with its shining blade is the beginning of my proposition.

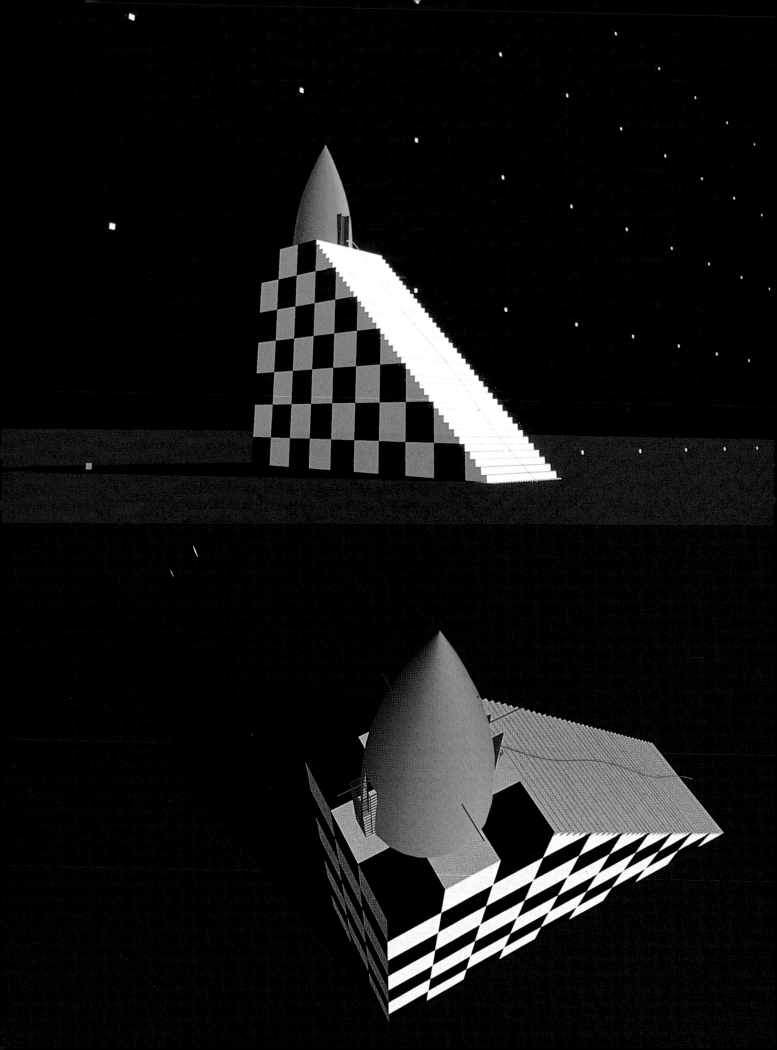

MOONDOG BUILDING, TOKYO – 'LA VIE DES BÊTES'

This monumental stairway made out of concrete, with plant ornaments, dominated by a green bronze rocket, is part of a residence in the centre of Tokyo.

Two regulations reign on this project: The first is that the inhabitant needs an effective relationship with his home. For this, an original shape is needed which will allow him to recognise it from a distance and, from then on, in the context of the street. The tie will start to be weaved that will reunify them – the link that will be reinforced by a territory feeling achieved in the elevation of the facade. The other approach, which is more symbolic, is the research of a poetic space left by fallen utopias. It is touching to see this in some of the illustrations in Jules Verne's books — how to the point the premises of his intuitions are, but how fragile they become in his trip through the history of form.

The Moondog building will try to express the poetry contained in the breaks between human dreams.

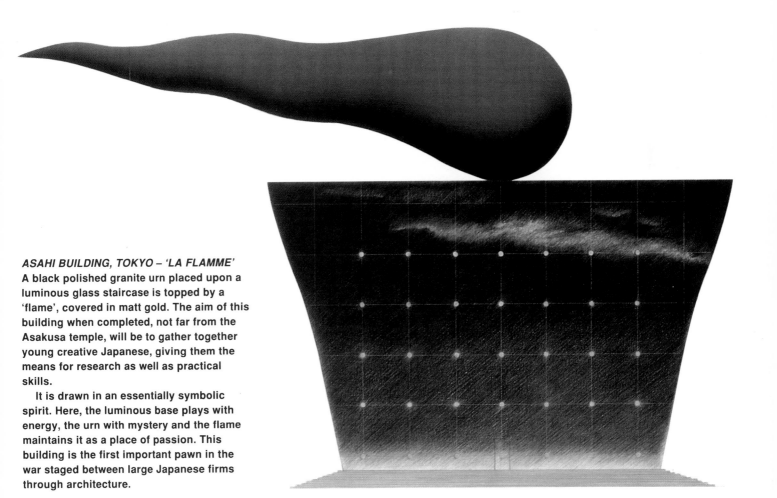

ASAHI BUILDING, TOKYO – 'LA FLAMME'
A black polished granite urn placed upon a luminous glass staircase is topped by a 'flame', covered in matt gold. The aim of this building when completed, not far from the Asakusa temple, will be to gather together young creative Japanese, giving them the means for research as well as practical skills.

It is drawn in an essentially symbolic spirit. Here, the luminous base plays with energy, the urn with mystery and the flame maintains it as a place of passion. This building is the first important pawn in the war staged between large Japanese firms through architecture.

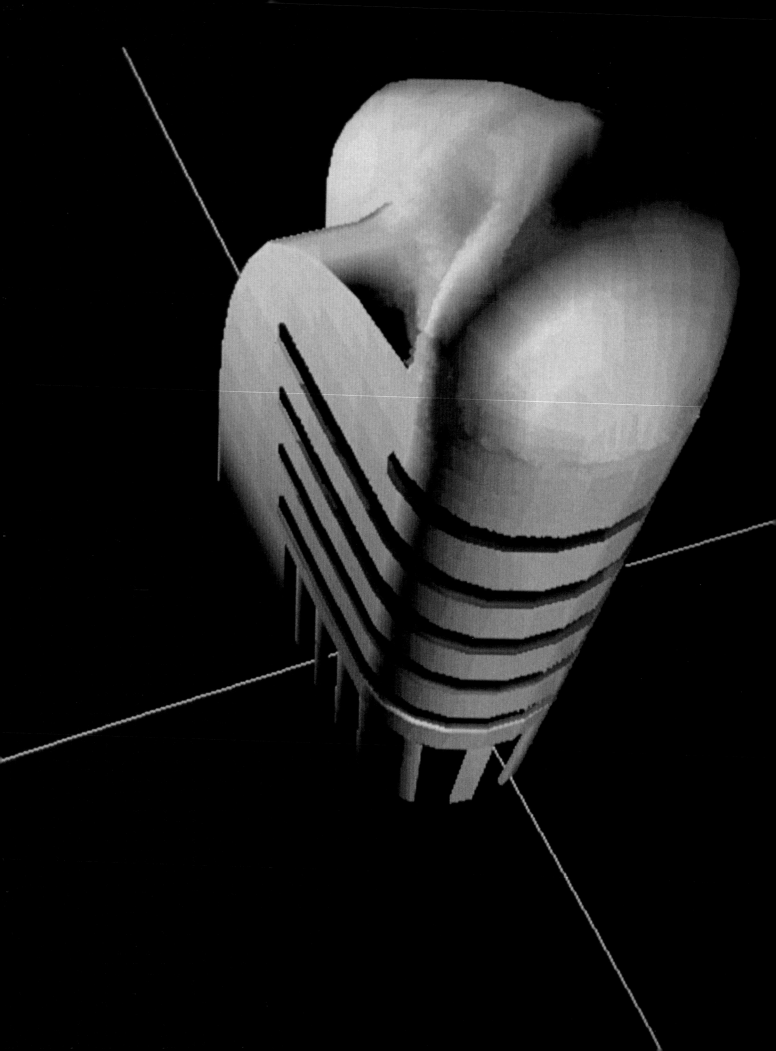

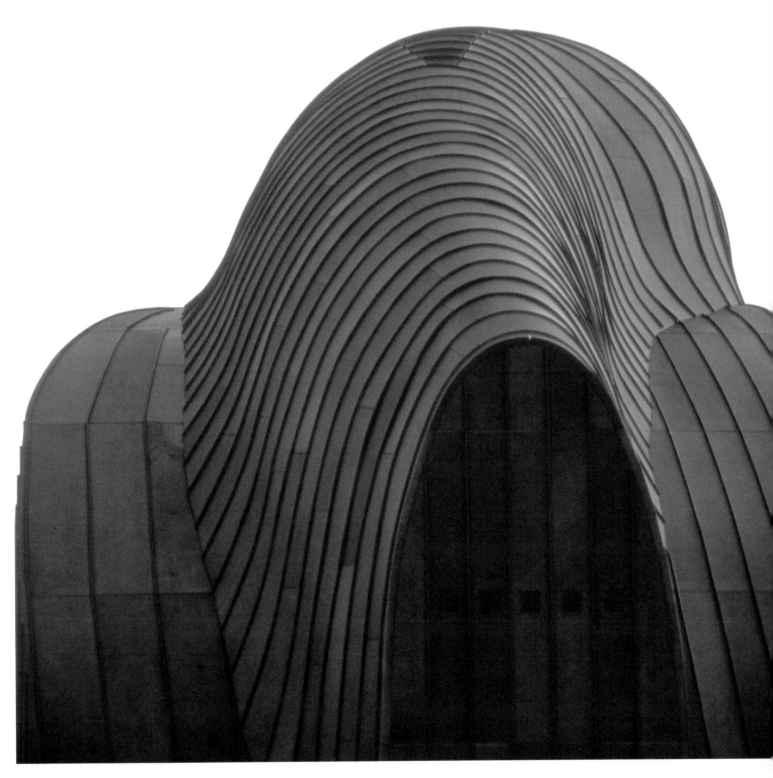

NANINANI BUILDING, TOKYO

In French, Naninani means the unnameable, without a name. To the Japanese, it is the cry exclaimed on seeing a ghost.

A biomorphic bronze monster trickling with green oxide looms up from the depths of the Japaneses' greatest fears, this building merits its title.

Naninani seeks to answer the question which makes use of our schooling: 'Do inanimate objects have a soul?'

Perhaps Naninani has a soul; in any case, it is the first living building.

The green oxide from which it is made permanently drips to the ground where, little by little, it will fill up the complicated network of arabesque faults. It will betray, after years have gone by, the organic origins of this building, where it is best not to stay alone at night.

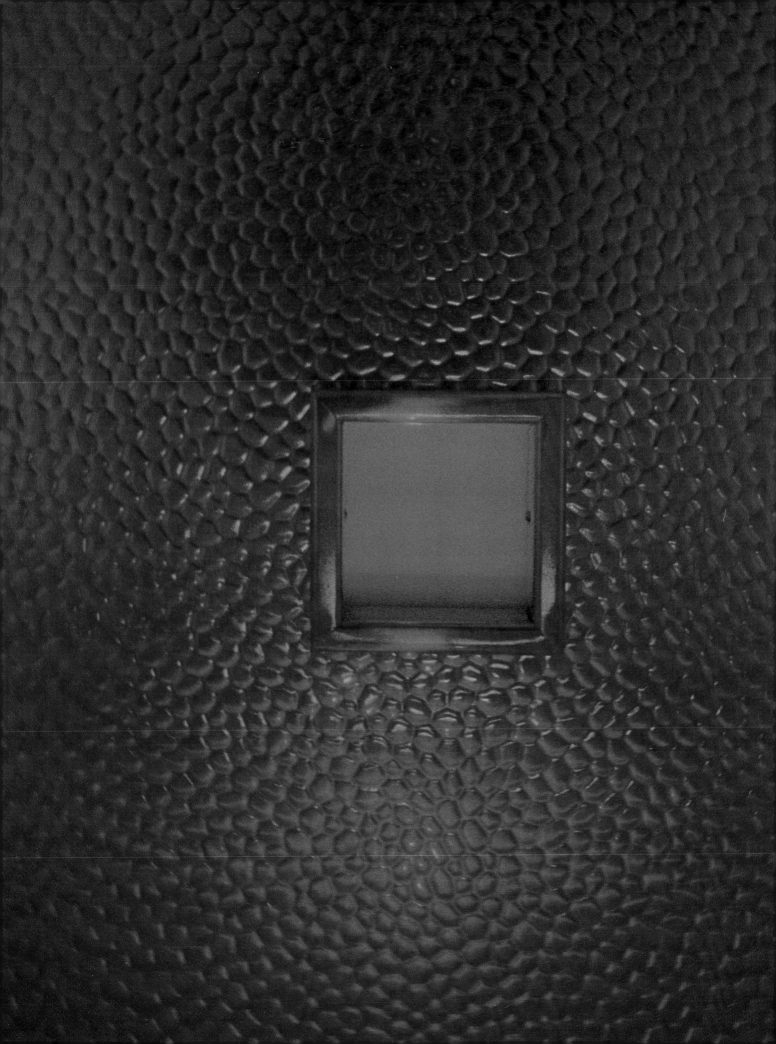

TEATRIZ RESTAURANT, MADRID
Situated right in the centre of Madrid, the Teatriz, which at the beginning of the century was a theatre, was blessed with a number of beautiful volumes. Therefore, the conversion called for delicate manipulation on the part of the architect . . . There were no, or nearly no, references left of the auditorium. The stage, however, was respected: 'For lack of architectural quality, the theatre here retains some beautiful traces from the past.' As Starck comments: 'This is the first time that I have managed to balance the parameters of fantasy, rigour and sympathy so well. The strong and novel idea for me was that one could give emotion whilst remaining friendly, make up fantasy whilst remaining rigorous, and create ambiguous places whilst remaining elegant. It is a juxtaposition of semantic touches. Whether this is beautiful or not does not concern me.'

OMA
CHECKPOINT CHARLIE

Elia Zenghelis, in an earlier description of this project, has made particular note of the dramatic shift in circumstances surrounding the building, which has now resulted in a change of use. Initially the collaboration between the military and the municipality of Kreuzberg, was a response to a shortage of social housing, Checkpoint Charlie intentionally echoes the forms of the Wall and viewing towers that were once so close to it. In response to that duality the ground floor was planned as a service faculty for allied troops and the upper levels were given over to apartments of various sizes. A distinct podium base, which separated these two functions, was intended to make the division between them clear. Direct meta-

phors such as the roof, which is clad in polished metal, and seems to fly over the building like an aeroplane wing continue this formal theme, and make an unmistakeable reference to specific events in the history of the city.

While the Wall has now been removed, this particular piece of real estate still evokes strong mental images of that past, which are undoubtedly amplified by several isolated structures from pre-war Berlin that still stand throughout the city. A painting of the Checkpoint Charlie project, by Zoe Zenghelis, has captured the essence of these images, with a cool grey and white palette being used to convey the complicated texture of the memories associated

with this gateway through the wall. While other paintings by Zenghelis have also featured architecture as the focal point of a depopulated world, the lifeless empty street that she shows here effectively communicates a silence of another sort.

Despite all its physical and metaphorical connections with the past, Checkpoint Charlie also contains an equally timely set of signs that allow it to escape purely contextual categorisation. By doing so, it manages to exemplify the irrepressible optimism that now pervades Berlin itself.

Architects: Elia Zenghelis and Matthias Sauerbruch with Dirk Alten, Barbara Burren, Eleni Gigantes, Reni Keller, Alex Wall

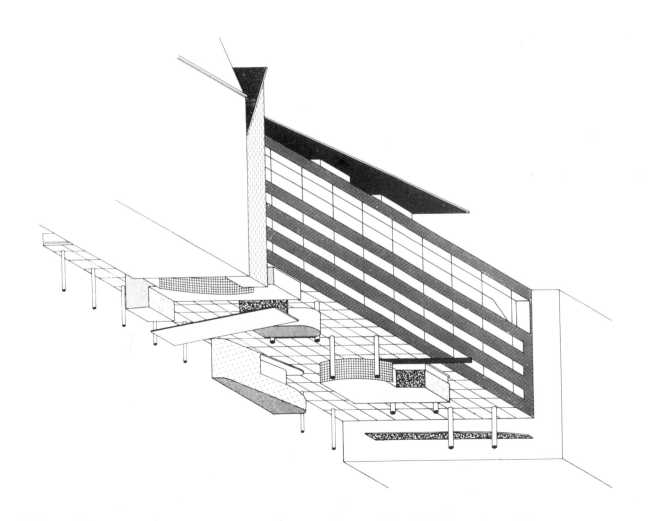

THE WILSON PARTNERSHIP WITH CHASSAY WRIGHT

BLACKBURN HOUSE, LONDON

Peter Wilson's concern in the furthering of directions in architecture has been widely appreciated over recent years. In the London mews house he develops his pioneering ideas for clients Janice and David Blackburn, both of whom have a strong involvement in the contemporary art world: Janice at the Saatchi Collection and David with the commissioning of art within the Broadgate office complex in the City of London. The brief for their house consisted of transforming a rundown range of prosaic mews buildings into two spaces for housing their own substantial collection of contemporary art and furniture – a gallery flat on the first and second floors above David's office on the ground floor. The architect explains: 'To cancel the original inconclusive volume a new white box was created (walls raised and windows closed). Each element added to this white frame tells its own story. The large window breaks out, the view is not good so the glass is opaque, blinded. Only fragmented views are available through small, clear areas of glass. A negative drawing on a window surface.

'The window shares the facade with the second practical opportunity, the Totem, a stainless steel and welded plastic column that carries clean water into the house and dirty water away. A guardian of entrance.

'Much of the architecture is on the level of interior detail. Door handles, supporting column and cantilevered balcony all in the same structural steel. A vitrine, a handrail in the middle of the upper gallery. Each piece has an autonomous narrative as well as a family resemblance to its neighbours through the use of a limited range of materials: tough steel, refined wood, one colour and the white of the box that contains them.

'The visitor only finally understands the house when he arrives at the top floor. This large, single space with a double-height void inside the big window is the gallery/living room. Light comes from above or near the floor, no views out are available but the space hovers.

'The back wall is entirely blank – for pictures. In the middle between dining and living space floats the Barge Seat. Sitting here, the visitor finally reaches the centre of the house – hovering like the house hovers, not quite part of London.'

We have interviewed Janice and David Blackburn and here they discuss the building and its contents.

JB: This was a building to house a collection of contemporary furniture craft and art pieces. We both found Peter Wilson a very exciting architect. However, he wasn't to dominate the contents of the building. His brief was very specific.

– How long have you been collecting and working closely with contemporary artists and architects?

JB: Collecting is something I've always done. I've commissioned things ever since I can remember, and long before I married David. As a developer, David has been involved with architects and we also know a lot of architects as friends. Commissioning adds an extra dimension. There is always a very interesting interplay between the client and the artist or craftsman which, if it is successful, makes the experience a very enjoyable one and adds to the pleasure we get from the finished piece. Having this house designed was an idea that

evolved and brought together all our interests in the field of contemporary arts and architecture.

– How did you choose Peter Wilson?

JB: My original choice was Piers Gough but he wasn't really free to take the job. I think that he thought we were only contemplating quite a simple conversion which he wasn't particularly interested in. He was also just finishing Janet Street-Porter's house and I don't think he really wanted to take on another house at that moment. I liked him very much as an architect and as a person and he told us about Peter Wilson. We then met Peter who very quickly understood what we were interested in and that we wanted to commission a piece of contemporary architecture as an extension of our interest in furniture and art as well as to house our collection.

– How did Peter Wilson feel about working with the idea of putting pieces of furniture and art into his spaces?

JB: He was very excited by it, even if he did not always like our choices. But, in general, he did not try to interfere. He never said 'This is appalling, you can't have it!'

DB: Our primary objective was always to create what we wanted to be an exciting contemporary setting for our contemporary things. So Peter understood the prospective relationship between his architecture and our collection from the outset. As the project developed we came to see the architecture as very much part and parcel of what we were collecting. In designing Peter had the advantage that we weren't planning to live in the gallery flat. We were certainly not building something that could not be lived in but we were able occasionally to go ahead with an idea that seemed to take us right up to the limit of practicability. Instead of saying 'That's just going to be too difficult to handle' we could hold on tight and say 'Let's go for it'.

JB: I think Peter liked the challenge. Even though we are both quite strong and have very definite ideas, everything was discussable and the plans for the furniture and art always added an additional dimension to the architectural issues. No idea was ever just rejected either by Peter or us. Eventually we agreed on almost everything. So it was a very good relationship. Most people don't have this kind of relationship with their architects – especially not after the job is finished. If Peter were living in England and we were to do another house I would certainly use him again.

– How did the essential concepts of the design evolve?

DB: I can give you two examples:

We decided at a very early stage, after a few discussions with Peter weighing up pros and cons, that we wanted to create a double-height space. The attraction was that we could have the opportunity of a very large feature window and create a dramatic sculptural volume which would impact on all the surrounding spaces. The downside was that there was very little floor space in the whole building and we were taking some of it away. We decided to sacrifice the floor space and get the benefit of the double-height. That was a very early 'joint' decision. The concept of creating the double-height space in the form of a volume skewed out from the basic box of the building was totally Peter's and was the first introduction to the design of the 15-degree angle which seems to be something of a 'signature' for him.

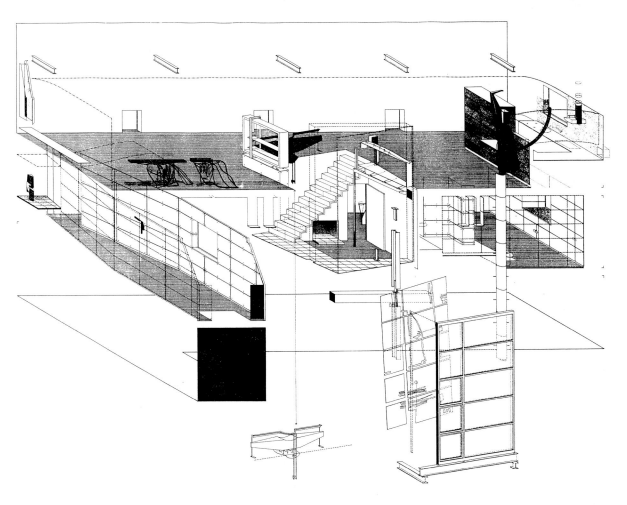

LEFT: LANDING WITH RUG BY ELIZABETH BROWNING-JACKSON, CHAIR BY JOHN MILLS AND CERAMIC BY CAROL MCNICOLL;
TOP LEFT: LANDING WITH PETER WILSON UMBRELLA STAND; *TOP RIGHT*: VIEW OF WINDOW IN STUDY;
OVERLEAF: STUDY SHOWING DESK BY FLORIS VAN DEN BROECKE AND CUPBOARDS BY PETER WILSON

The study on the first floor was a case of making a virtue out of necessity. The constraints of the site and the basic form of the building envelope left us with what seemed a hopelessly narrow room. We were inclined to despair. Peter's response was to make the room even narrower! He resorted again to the 15-degree angle theme and simply created two wedge-shaped volumes which he removed from the room to form cupboards along approximately half the length of the long sides. The result was a dramatic bottle-shaped space which he further accentuated by placing a floor to ceiling slot window at the narrow end.

– How much of the furniture in the house did Peter Wilson design?

DB: Peter designed an impressive range of widely differing pieces in a variety of materials – the Barge Seat, vitrine, cassette cupboard and Hi-Fi shelf in the top floor living area, the kitchen cooker hood, the terrazzo washbasin vanitory unit and shower tray in the bathroom, the built-in ranges of cupboards in the study, bedroom and kitchen, and the 'guard dog' umbrella stand. In addition, he designed a whole range of shelves, steps, handrails and door handles all of which are beautifully detailed and integrated into the 'total design'. He did not even stop short of pure decoration and himself had the idea of applying coloured embellishment to 'customise' the standard production dining chairs.

JB: He could easily have designed all the furniture and I think that he would have loved to have done so – very much in the tradition of Mackintosh or Frank Lloyd Wright. In a way, he was probably frustrated by the fact that we were so interested in commissioning and selecting ourselves as our taste is in many respects quite opposed to his. Had we wanted to leave everything to him I am sure it would have been beautiful as well – but very different.

For me, one of his best pieces was the cassette cupboard which is brilliant. We needed a cupboard but I wanted something which didn't look like one. I thought the cupboard should be very innocuous. My idea was to have something that hid itself away. Instead he designed a cupboard (and the shelf and fitment for the Hi-Fi) which actually became the feature of one end of the living area. It really is a sculpture. It is the opposite of what I had in mind and far better.

– Was the cupboard specifically designed to go in that corner?

DB: Yes. The ceiling curves downwards and there is a slot adjacent to it that leads up to a roof-light running the length of the space. Part of the brilliance of Peter's design is that he didn't stop the cupboard just below the ceiling line. Instead he took it right up so that it actually rises slightly above the curved ceiling and protrudes into the slot with a rather cheeky steel flourish.

– How did the staircase come about? Whose idea was that initially?

DB: This was one of Peter's best inspirations. It obviously evolved from the form and positioning of the double-height space which led to the staircase being skewed relative to the main front and rear walls of the building and positioned to 'sit' across the internal wall at first-floor level parallel to them. Once inside the double-height space you are really not aware of the peculiarity but before entering it the underside of a tapering portion of the staircase makes a strong visual impact reading very much as a sculptural element. To understand it immediately you must either be a pretty accomplished architect or walk straight through into the double-height space and see that the form which has just attracted your attention is actually a part of the underside of the staircase on the other side.

– Are there any other features of the design that particularly excited you in the early stages?

DB: We always loved the idea for the Totem which Peter unveiled very early in our discussions. The concept underlying the 'drawing' on the large feature window was very attractive from the outset but in retrospect I don't think that we fully appreciated its quality as a piece of art in its own right until we eventually saw the completed detailed drawing. The repeated uses of materials such as slate and steel in different contexts throughout the building attracted us from very early in the design process as did the way in which the curved range

of sycamore veneered kitchen cupboards cuts through the plane of the slate separating the kitchen from the dining area, linking the two spaces.

– How do you see Peter Wilson's furniture pieces, especially given that you do not use the house for living in? Do you think that he thought of the furniture he designed – the cassette cupboard for instance – as being a piece of art, or both a piece of art and a functional piece of furniture?

DB: I am sure that he regards pieces such as the cassette-cupboard, the Barge Seat, the vitrine, the kitchen cooker hood, and the terrazzo elements in the bathroom as integral parts of the architecture, having at the same time very strong sculptural qualities and quite definite utilitarian functions. To me, they represent a varied group of lively and witty examples of applied art actually bringing all these aspects together. I think that Peter may simply view them as some of the more obvious examples of the wealth of architectural detailing with which he filled the project.

– Did Peter Wilson know which pieces of furniture were to go in whilst you were planning the house?

DB: We always told him whatever we actually happened to be doing in terms of commissioning or buying. Some of the things we were working on or had bought he certainly wouldn't have chosen himself but he was very enthusiastic indeed about others. In some cases he became quite actively involved with us in debating both the designs of the pieces themselves and their relationships with the architecture.

JB: The piece of furniture that Peter was most closely involved with was perhaps Ron Arad's dining table which turned out to be the first of a family of tables that Ron did although it was very different from anything he had done before. The table was a true collaboration between us, Ron and Peter. I liked Ron's work very much and Peter knew him from the AA. We wanted a table which would be reasonably restrained by Ron's standards at that time. We have stayed in close touch with Ron and continue to commission work from him.

DB: I think there was a particularly strong affinity between Peter and Ron because Peter himself works so well with steel which is Ron's principal material. Their collaboration on the dining table ended up with Peter adding a light set into the floor to his design to achieve the full effect of the sandwiched steel and honeycomb aluminium within the glass top.

JB: On the other hand, some of our commissions involved us in a lot of detailed work with craftsmen totally independent of Peter. For example, having created the top floor space, we were talking to Elizabeth Browning-Jackson – an established furniture and textile designer in New York – about rugs. A spiral looked interesting and together we had the idea of adding elements coming up the stairs and leading along the narrow 'path' to the living area. We had seen some examples of Elizabeth's work where she had developed a theme of creating an effect of a staircase through the use of contrasting colours and shapes within the fabric of a rug. An early idea was for a rug in three parts: a spiral, a central section, and a section going all the way down the stairs. The stair section proved quite tricky and eventually we decided that it would probably be dangerous so we ended up with two sections. The whole rug exercise involved endless discussions with Elizabeth whom we visited two or three times when we were in New York. We were in constant correspondence and David was also sending her floor plans. It was a protracted and complicated long-distance design exercise for a very site specific piece.

– Can you imagine ever replacing the contemporary artwork and furniture chosen with the house in mind, or will everything stay as it is?

DB: In design or aesthetic terms I certainly don't see everything as frozen. Very few of the pieces that weren't 'built-in' by Peter are totally site specific (in the sense either that we would not like them if they were elsewhere, or that others could not be substituted for them). Having said that, almost every one was commissioned or

LEFT: LANDING WITH CHAIR BY FORREST MYERS;
ABOVE: VIEW OF BEDROOM AND ENTRY TO BATHROOM, WITH BED BY FRED BAIER

LEFT AND ABOVE: LANDING BY WINDOW SHOWING TABLE AND CHAIR BY BOB TROTMAN

VIEW OF SECOND FLOOR SHOWING BARGE SEAT BY PETER WILSON, ARMCHAIR BY JASPER MORRISON AND VASE BY SYDNEY HUTTER

DETAILED VIEW OF SECOND FLOOR SHOWING PAINTING BY BEN NICHOLSON, *ONE CURVE, ONE CIRCLE*

LEFT: DINING AREA SHOWING RON ARAD TABLE; *ABOVE LEFT*: KITCHEN SHOWING BRUCE MCLEAN SCULPTURE *ABOVE RIGHT*: DETAIL SHOWING WORK BY MICHAEL CRAIG-MARTIN; *OVERLEAF*: LIVING AREA WITH RUG BY ELIZABETH BROWNING-JACKSON, TABLE BY BRUCE MCLEAN, CHAIR BY SCOTT BURTON, WORK BY ANDY WARHOL, SOFA BY JASPER MORRISON AND CASSETTE CABINET AND HI-FI FITMENT BY PETER WILSON

acquired with a particular location in mind and to interact in terms of form, material and colour with others. We have always seen the grouping and bringing together of the pieces as an added bonus. The prospect of rearrangement and substitution is very exciting. I'm sure that as time passes it will open up a whole new range of aspects and implications of the architecture.

– *Could you tell us a little about the ground floor?*

DB: My original involvement with the building was when I just leased two of the ground floor rooms for my office and had the interior of them designed by David Davies. David did an excellent (but necessarily limited) job designing behind what was then a most uninspiring exterior. More than two years later after I had acquired the whole building I decided to incorporate the remainder of the ground floor into the office to create a suite of four conventionally-shaped interconnecting rooms. When Peter became involved, his design of course treated the structure and elevation in a completely integrated manner although he was only involved to a very limited extent with the internal ground floor layout. He did however contribute two very distinctive metal radiator covers. They sound very minor, but to me they are definite links with the rest of the building in terms of architectural detail. Despite the need for the office to be highly functional and completely self-contained we have enjoyed extending our contemporary furniture and art collection into it and it now feels very much 'of a piece' with the gallery flat.

– *Having had time to reflect after completing this house how do you feel about the possibility of doing another?*

JB: I would love to start again. I feel we were in many ways experimenting and learning. We have dreamed of building a contemporary house in the country. All we need is the right piece of land, planning permission, and an enthusiastic architect with plenty of time.

– *Having been involved in the Broadgate development, how do you approach putting works of art in a semi-public environment where people work as opposed to a house where only guests and friends will see them?*

DB: Putting art into an environment like Broadgate involves many considerations. You've got a lot of different interests to keep in mind: thousands of people just walking through every day; the tenants paying the rent whose corporate images are closely related to the buildings and their surroundings, their Boards of Directors, employees who travel back and forth and work in the offices day in and day out, and the whole gamut of their clients and visitors; and then of course the planners and public interest groups ranging from the Royal Fine Art Commission to the most parochial local watchdog committee.

Naturally, there is an element of trying to please everyone. But at the same time you know that if you are not simply going to avoid anything which may be in any way controversial, you can only exercise your best judgement (which will necessarily be subjective and reflect your own taste) whilst at the same time being sensitive to all the various different considerations and interests.

From this standpoint, decisions on the introduction of art into an urban working environment are not different in kind from decisions which a developer has to take on questions of architectural taste. They just create an additional dimension in the sense that until relatively recently art was all too frequently regarded as an optional extra (and even, perhaps, something of an affectation) in the development context. Developers have become very used to taking architectural decisions after listening to views, taking on board points from all directions, and responding to what seem to be the relevant issues – commercial, aesthetic, and even occasionally moral. Ultimately, it is the developer who has to decide what building he builds. The considerations involved in introducing art are very similar – the main differences being that art stimulates an even greater diversity of individual opinions than architecture and the whole process is that much less familiar because the vast majority of buildings are built without incorporating any art at all.

Personally, I believe that all aesthetic decisions are generally better made by a single individual or a very small group than in large committees. In the particular context of choosing art for working environments and public places, there is a very real conflict between the pressure to follow a conventional, structured business approach and the conviction that the larger the decision making group and the more formalised the process the less satisfactory the outcome is likely to be. It's not so much a matter of fear of taking a bad decision as frustration that an opportunity to do something of real quality may be lost.

For me, the high point of the Broadgate art programme was Richard Serra's sculpture: *Fulcrum*. Quite apart from being a great admirer of Richard's work I felt committed from the outset to the appropriateness of *Fulcrum* for Broadgate and its particular location within it. The work was specifically designed for the space with the architecture of the surrounding buildings very much in mind. The relationship between Richard Serra and the architect (Peter Foggo), had much in common with the collaboration between Ron Arad and Peter Wilson although the context was of course much broader and more complex. It is well known that buildings can take a long time to become familiar and establish themselves within a broader environment and I suspect that art may take even longer. It is perhaps not surprising that the initial debate provoked by Richard Serra's work was at a very simplistic level: would five steel plates be more appropriate in a shipyard then the City of London? The real test will, I think, come in several years' time when *Fulcrum* has become accepted and acknowledged as an integral part of Broadgate and the questions being addressed are whether it is or is not a major work of art, whether its importance as a sculpture derives in any way from its siting, and whether its presence contributes to Broadgate in any more significant way than that of an item of street furniture. I am confident that it will pass the test with flying colours and look forward to being around when it does.

Having waxed lyrical about a particular piece of art I must also say that I did not see the Broadgate challenge in art terms as being to create a first class sculpture park which just happened to be within a City development. If that had been our prime purpose we could well have ended up with more 'important' art but Broadgate would have been a far less successful and agreeable working urban environment. I am convinced that there is a real difference between achieving the very topical objective of the marriage between art and architecture and simply exposing art to the public in and around buildings.

HAUS RUCKER CO
RECENT PROJECTS BY ZAMP KELP

'The annihilation of the object which one finds in the abstract concepts of modern art becomes reality in the actual social space by virtue of media projection. . . . Architecture has to change. As a link between reality and projection of the media it remains true to its nature – creating space for the organisation of society. At the same time it will have to take into account the fact that its image together with social events have to play an important role in the projective part of our world.' *Heinrich Klotz*

ORNAMENTA 1: BUILT FICTION EXHIBITION , PFORZHEIM 1989

Ornamenta 1 was an exhibition which presented jewellery, for the most part, as art in miniature and in so doing claimed the conceptual openness which is appropriate to a World Exhibition of Jewellery.

The fact that there were a limited number of exhibition rooms available determined the design of the exhibition structure. A formation of blue cubes penetrated and superimposed the exhibition building, disregarding the existing space limits. The pilasters were all the same dimension and were symmetrically placed within a network aligned to the proportions of the exhibition building.

The blue cubes were conceived as media eclipsing the normal situation, being outlined volumes, which in their inner spatiality were of indefinite dimensions.

They were designed to reveal themselves to the visitor of the exhibition through openings in the outer skin which projected their imaginary and concrete contents via video monitors to the outside.

In the pilasters the jewellery was given the impression of weightlessness – gliding; a large number of artistic highlights designed for the cosmos of our everyday life.

Analogous to the monolith in Kubrick's film '2001, A Space Odyssey', which gives intelligence to those who touch it, the formation of the blue cubes pretended to be able to appear at different times and places to deliver the message of a civilisation being revalued by the culture of jewellery.

MEKKA MEDIAL
GARE D'AUSTERLITZ, PARIS 1989

Analogous to the oriental town Mecca, which is both religious strong point and cultural centre of the Arabic world, Mekka Medial is a centre for cultural processes and perspectives in Europe. Instead of religious elements, we find here studies based around media technological phenomena, which often reach religious dimensions in society.

Mekka Medial consists of 40 cubic spaces, which are opened on their topside. These spaces give room for the generation and disappearance of different scenerios. The principal item of the installation is a mobile cube, which can be manipulated over each of the potential environments on the ground. This cube functions mainly as a mobile events hall, open on its underside and thus completing the scenerio. This Mobile Kaaba also houses a broadcasting station and administration areas. Like a Queen Bee taking care of the honeycombs of its hive, the Mobile Kaaba cares and controls the 40 spaces over which it hovers. Over an integrated TV-Channel, the activities and identities of Mekka Medial become perceptible all over Europe.

Every European should visit Mekka Medial at least once in a lifetime, to realise the relationships between medial projection and the geographical place of genesis.

In doing that, the visitors will meet a great number of people coming from different parts of the continent who have all gone on a pilgrimage for the similar reason, to see the sources of medial projection produced by Mekka Medial and to participate directly on a permanent communicative medial event.

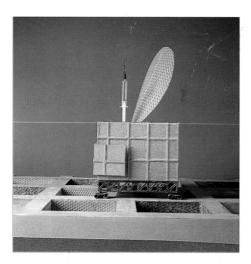

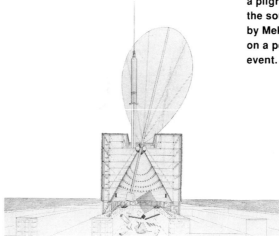

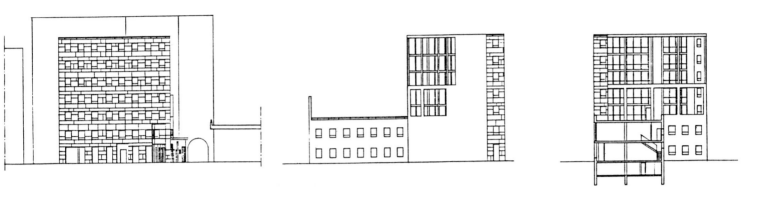

UHLANDSTRASSE 18-19
BERLIN 1985-89

This building, being the last in a row of houses, has to volumetrically expand into the street and additionally on to a communications structure, the city's railway line, which crosses the Uhlandstrasse. These considerations lead to a corner solution with a compact appearance, when viewed from the public area of the vacant space. Inside the block, however, the cube is bevelled and opens diagonally through glass and metal constructions towards the southwest. A blue wall (4m in height) with a ceramic coating projects from the building and visually eases the architectural eye-sores which exist opposite the railway line. Simultaneously, the existing passage between Uhlandstrasse and Grolmannstrasse is rendered visible.

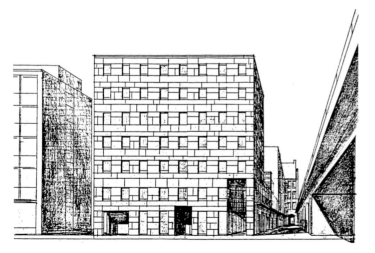

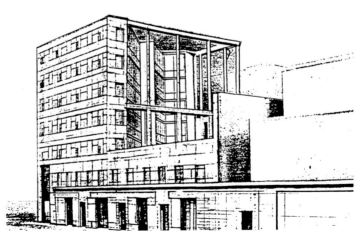

*Bruce Graham of Skidmore, Owings
and Merrill, Boots Pure Drug
Corporate Headquarters, Nottingham,
1968.*

EZRA STOLLER
PHOTOGRAPHS OF ARCHITECTURE

Ezra Stoller's photographs of architecture are great unexpected treasures of the last half century of photography. The extraordinary quality of insight and perception they offered from the start of Stoller's career in 1939 remained unnoticed by most critics, historians, and Stoller himself until the late 1970s because Stoller never worked or was asked to work as an artist (although he has been an outstanding one). He was perceived as the consummate professional-for-hire, a craftsman with a job to do who would do it with special care and skill. So he was a hero among the small community of architectural photographers and the best man for the job among architects seeking images of their work.

A Stoller picture is stripped of all distractions. It goes straight for the jugular, with some of the ferocious energy that phrase implies. There is no dead spot, no less than optimal light, no cheap effect, no fake prettiness. A key strength of the building is seen and seized. Stoller has, in fact, a sort of tunnel vision, excluding much in order to see much, in utter concentration.

When photographers recognise 'a Stoller', they see phenomenal technique apparent in unerring sharpness of focus at all distances at once, in the capturing of extraordinary detail, and in a simple, balanced, classical composition of unquestionable good taste. They want to know how he did it, what his secret tricks were. But there were no tricks. Stoller rightly claims to be uninterested in technique and technology except as tools to express his interest in architecture. The familiar clarity, sobriety, simplicity, and sharpness of his compositions are necessary by-products of his determination to *see*, clearly and sharply, what he calls the 'idea' of a building. Unlike technique, such seeing cannot be taught.

Since Stoller as an artist (a person who makes a world meaningful through the objective embodiment of his feeling response to it) is more like a critic (devoted to understanding what he is not) than like a dreamer (expressing what he is within a fancied otherness) we may be slow to see how, like all artists, he opens up worlds to us in a personal way. He would like us to think that he is effaced and disinterested. This, in a sense, he is, but it is precisely this passionate devotion to the essence of buildings that gives his work a personal, interested cast and its artistic depth.

His is a world coloured by feelings of sober but profound pleasure, excitement, firm tactile holding and concentration, of loving and seizing the object in the same gesture. It is very different from Judith Turner's world of obscure, private abstractions of architectural details (which have their own dreamlike strength). It is anti-Romantic. It is Cézanne looking hard and long at Mont St Victoire, not Chagall imagining his wife flying to kiss him. It is, however, the Romantic sort, not Stoller's classical sort, that we too

automatically associate with 'real' art. And the Romantic artist would never work as a hireling serving other people's goals.

Architectural photography in the normal sense of a business and communication service for architects and publications, is obligated to be object, not self, centred. Yet most architectural photography in magazines is dull and unrevealing not because it is too subjective but because the building has not been seen by a strong and vital person who brings it to life through his own vitality. A dull spirit sees dully. It can be argued that overly subjective architectural photography includes the all-too-common glamorising photography that imposes pretty light or colour or distorting angles to make weak buildings seem powerful. Since no honest self is at work, we have neither true subject nor true object, but mere rhetoric, designed for theatrical effect, which Stoller despises.

Yet time and again Stoller himself is said to 'make buildings look better than they are' (among others Paul Rudolph and Myron Goldsmith have said this to me; Arthur Drexler has written it). In some sense this is true, and it represents the most serious criticism of Stoller's approach. Stoller does not give us an accurate representation, or anything like it, of something we need to know: the mundane, daily experience of buildings, warts and all, in their context, disturbed by people, furniture, rain, other buildings, and cars. He does not tell us what it is like to work in the office towers or to see the cracks in Fallingwater's balconies. His record is not for historians, anthropologists, or sociologists. It may even not be inclusive enough for architecture historians. Stoller was not hired to tell the whole story and he does not do so. But he does tell one true story wholly: the real ideal of the building.

For a gritty, cynical man, Stoller is a surprisingly pure idealist. What Stoller sees in a building is its implicit spiritual/corporeal ideal: what it is striving to be as actually present in what it is. Stoller says frequently that 'photography is not reality'. He is not naive on that score. But in being honest – which he believes it can be – photography is pointing towards part of reality. Stoller is firmly opposed to forcing into a faked-up picture what is not there, yet he is also morally opposed to allowing the building's aesthetic weaknesses, dead spots, and technical or social shortcomings obstruct a view of its real best 'self'. This is what makes him the honourable architect's perfect servant: No lies, but also no attention paid to anything except what the architect consciously or unconsciously cares about most deeply.

There is a problem (aside from the neglect of the user's ordinary experience) with this approach that Stoller is well aware of: an essence, an ideal, of a building may be absent, trivial, ignoble, dull, or unintelligent. When Stoller finds this in his subjects, his pictures look like any ordinary

Frank Lloyd Wright, Johnson Administration Building and Research Tower, Racine, Wisconsin, 1944. The building was to be seen as a tree with its floor-like branches, cantilevered from the central trunk.

James Stirling, History Building, Cambridge University, England, 1964.

*Myron Goldsmith of Skidmore,
Owings and Merrill, Solar Telescope,
Kitt Peak, Arizona, 1962, 'I felt the
need to understand the workings of
this telescope and tried to include that
understanding implicitly in my
photographs. . . . In a far-off valley to
the right of the photograph is an
Indian village which provided an
exciting contrast of scale with the
telescope.'*

Philip Johnson, Johnson House, New Canaan, Connecticut, 1949. A not very practical, Mies-influenced house that provided a good framework for Johnson's art collection.

Eero Saarinen (with Smith, Hinchman and Grylls), General Motors Technical Center, Warren, Michigan, 1950. Photographed before Dan Kiley's landscaping was completed.

photographer's: clear and straightforward but lifeless. As Stoller says, 'You can't have great architectural photography without great architecture.' Luckily for Stoller and us, Stoller has lived when there were several great or near great architects who wanted him to cover their work or whose work magazines or corporations hired him to shoot. His career begins when Modernism was taking off in America (the late 30s), matures in the late 50s (I think of 1958-68, when he was 43-53 years old, as his glory decade) and moves towards retirement near the birth of Post-Modernism and the Late-Modern work of Pei and Meier.

Stoller's ability to see and seize the ideal of a building was no doubt, reinforced through his own undergraduate architectural training at New York University and in his mingling with Modern architects during his regular visits to the Harvard University Graduate School of design in the late 30s to see friends from NYU who were being taught by Gropius and Breuer. Stoller claims he is a failed architect (and adds, echoing Goethe's epigram about editors and writers, 'so are most architects'), but through his lens he sees what architects like to see: straight-on elevations, the shapings and relationships of space, important structural elements, innovations, and the relationship to the site when that matters. But he does not respect decoration and ornament, which are obviously important to fine architects. He considers these features decadent overlay, trivial in comparison to space and form, and inappropriate, given modern materials like glass and steel. The simplicity and boldness of his photographic grasp were drawn out best by Modern buildings' bold simple forms, not by older, more intricate, and decorated architecture.

Stoller's training as an architect is revealed in his choice of vantage points and emphases, which resemble those common in architects' drawings. . .

Stoller is unlike an architect, however, in that he must avoid creating artistic worlds with the character he would like them to have. Stoller has compared himself with a musician who is given a score and must bring it to life by performing it. He contrasts this to the critic who must make judgements. A performer must make the piece be as good as it can be. He cannot make a bad piece good, but he can draw out the strengths in a piece that has strengths. The comparison is fitting. And just as a good performer must be able to play sympathetically Bartok as well as Mozart, Stoller's *métier* makes his capacious, empathic response to diversity crucial. Philip Trager, a deliberately artistic architectural photographer of equally exquisite craftsmanship and taste, takes pictures more as the composer than as the performer – his work is quite prominently unified by his Hopper-like sensibility that casts a ghostly quality over all he sees. But for the job of architectural photography, it is not composers but performers that are most needed. Stoller's capaciousness is evident when one realises the same man took the masterful pictures of both Taliesin West and the Seagram Building, both Eero Saarinen's TWA Terminal at New York's John F Kennedy International Airport and Philip Johnson's Glass House in New Canaan, Connecticut.

Stoller not only works hard to avoid indulgent self-expression, he also is constantly pushing against the limitations of his medium, in this case its two-dimensionality, that which most dramatically distinguishes it from the architecture itself. He is quite aware that there can be no substitute for being in a building if it is to be known, and he is aware that people 'know' buildings more through pictures than through visits. For his 21st birthday, his wife-to-be Helen gave Stoller a book of Atget's photography. Stoller marks this event as the birth of his desire to be an architectural photographer. Atget appealed to Stoller because of his spontaneous honesty and devotion to his subjects, but it was primarily Atget's ability to bring the third dimension into his pictures that struck Stoller. Atget's many one-point perspectives of long streets and his use of reflections on glass storefronts to show there was a 'behind' as well as an 'in front' quickened Stoller's conviction that something in spirit architectural could be achieved on a flat piece of paper.

Stoller used several means, some of which have become magazine clichés, to increase the sense of pictorial depth. The most straightforward was to use one-point perspectives: long rooms, walkways, halls, or building edges plunging toward a vanishing point near the centre of the picture. . .

Generally, the first sunny day Stoller was at a site he would walk around and through the building for hours, gathering impressions, feelings, and thoughts, sometimes in company with the architect. The architect would tell him what he thought was important, but Stoller the loner would take it with a grain of salt, seeing what he saw and recording it on a rough plan drawing. This plan sketch would get more complex as the day wore on: Arrows would mark the best vantage point for a view. Eventually a time would be written by an arrow when it became clear which light would best serve that view. Any distracting mess – uneven window blinds, unstacked firewood – would be staightened. For interior shots, Stoller would remove or rearrange furniture to better co-operate with the architecture. A plan for interior supplementary lighting would be thought through. This was the time for the bulk of Stoller's creative work. The next day or days, except for the capturing of fortuitous coincidences, he would follow the mapped out plans and give them the refinements of inch-by-inch camera adjustments. The bedrock of Stoller's skill was the quality of his choice of vantage points and of light . . .

In his most strictly architectural photographs, Stoller's strengths are channelled to best use in two basic types: those that offer finished, grasping perceptions of rich, complex, and delightful spaces and those that present strong, classical, head-on elevations in such a way as to thrust up the sheer otherness of the buildings as revelations, like the sudden view of a grand antlered deer in a forest . . .

And finally, look back to Stoller's first important architectural photograph, taken when he was 32 years old, of Gropius and Breuer's Chamberlain Cottage, Wayland, Massachusetts. Of this house, Stoller has written, 'To me this little gem says everything that these giants of architecture had to say and does so better than most of the giant projects that they were destined to do later.' Strength through humility and honesty, restraint and directness. Two wood boxes mounted on stone, with two echoing openings each, exalted by the trees and sky to which they open themselves. A house linked to the high clouds by the great pine that Stoller carefully included in full. A house that embodies Stoller's own strengths as a working photographer, devoting himself for half a century, with fervour and rigour, to the achievements of others and thereby, through the very rejection of self-importance, becoming, to our surprise and lasting indebtness, the chief enabler of our experiences of Modern architecture.

William S Saunders

Philip Johnson, Kahn and Jacobs, Seagram Building, New York City. 1958. The razing of old apartment buildings on Park Avenue allowed unobstructed views of the Seagram building.

Myron Goldsmith Skidmore, Owings and Merrill, Equibank, Pittsburgh, Pennsylvania, 1975.

This article is based on an extract from William S Saunders' book Modern Architecture – Photographs by Ezra Stoller, *published by Harry N Abrams, New York. It is reproduced here by kind permission of the publishers.*

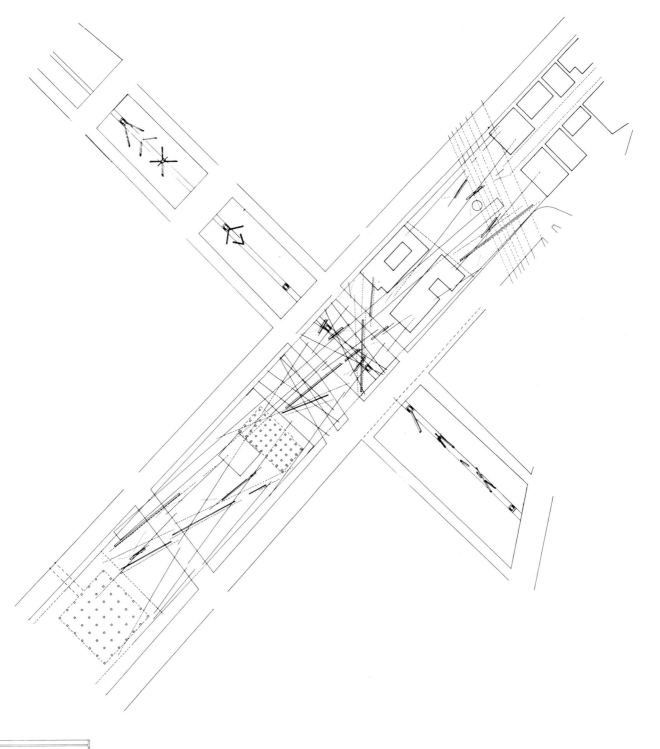

STEEL CLOUD, WEST COAST GATEWAY, LOS ANGELES

HANI RASHID
OPTIGRAPHS AND OTHER WRITING

A microchip of an infinitesimal dimension has been devised that will alter the commodity of history. Imagine if you will, a memory exchange containing all of history, all information and all means of knowing. In such a place one could barter and trade thought, diminish certain stocks while increasing the value of others. At each moment the exchange alters a 'Virtual Reality' while promoting random access memory (RAMS), thereby describing a history of supply and demand.

As the millenium recedes into the past, a 'new world order' of some unknown dimension is being concocted. A defunct 'cold' war has given way to the 'hot' battlefield of rewriting history. Television monitors, cam-corders and a 'sound-bite-diplomacy' are 'realities' to be reckoned with as the leisure society is replaced by an information civilisation.

ON RECENT NON-EVENTS
On eventual architecture
Those ignominious machines produce lean (fat-free) buildings. IMPROVED PLANS FOR IMPOVERISHED SOULS:
Procedure one: All surfaces including the screen and key-pad are to be painted then scraped, as one would dull claws against granite skin. Now with palate knife in hand scrawl the face of a goat peering from beyond the viscous monitor. STOP. These are the interminable vapours of convention, the *purgatory* of quality.
HYGIENIC ARCHITECTURE FOR THE CIVILISED in an age of detachment and indifference the burlesque of progress seems to endure all. Within this absence of reverie, the city is again engulfed in a 'constructed' plague where efficiency is but a *symptom* and *effect* the malady.
— Into that viscous black sea that swallowed Venice first fell the fit and soon after the docile —
AN ARCHITECTURE OF AMNESIA — ANAEMIC ARCHITECTURE
Marinetti locomotive has derailed! NO more revisions for revising is a duty for idiots. Enigma is only order and consensus an obscenity. Automobiles will undoubtedly persevere to incise the terrain with the keen deliberation of an *executioner*.
Procedure two: Tear then shred the conformists' cloak. The tarnished kid gloves of progress are to be tended to, cleaned and polished. Then along with technology discard all into the gutter!

OPTIGRAPH
Positions: (excerpts)
1 Standing or situated in front of; facing; as the house across the way is directly opposite to this.
3 In logic, differing in quantity or quality, or in both as propositions.
5 The act of opposing; attempt to check, restrain or defeat resistance.
9 In rhetoric a figure whereby two things are joined which seem incompatible. The kings have only one vacant square between them.
— Fight, attack, oppose, resist.
Criteria:
(Gr opsris, sight, and metron, measure.)
To choose; to wish for; to desire; by desire. Expressing desire or wish. An organ of sight; an eye.
(a) the angle included between the two lines drawn from the two extremities of an object to the centre of a lens tend to meet at some distance before the eyes.
(b) an instrument used in surveying, for laying out lines in right angles to each other. It consists of

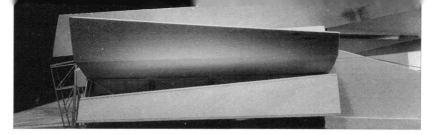

MOSCOW THEATRE, HERMITAGE GARDENS, MOSCOW

a circular brass box containing an index and horizon glasses, fixed at an angle of 45 degrees.
op' ti-graph, (Gr optikos, of seeing, and graphein, to write.)
1 A telescope made for the purpose of copying landscapes.
2 An instrument for producing pictures on a screen.
3 An instrument for measuring the limits of vision and the determining of imperfection.
4 The measure of capacity, the turning of the mind to that which has already occupied it.

A polished surface of metal or any other material suitable for reflecting rays of light, being converted into a cone on entering the lens and issuing as a hollow cylinder. The consequent producing of two distinct images. Terrestial objects appear to be farther from the horizon than they are in reality.

An optical instrument employed in viewing distant objects and terrain. It assists the architect in two ways; first, by enlarging the visual angle under which some distant object is seen and thereby manipulating the objects scale, and secondly by collecting and conveying to the eye a larger scope of possibilities:
— the object is inverted
— lenses which by successive refraction achieve the desired affect.
— A mechanism for moving the apparatus to keep it within the field of exploration.
— An instrument used for producing an appearance of relief in the objects of a landscape.

Nothing stands in the way of making use of complex APPARATUS such as film, automobile, lift, aeroplane, and other machinery, as well as optical instruments, reflecting equipment and so on . . . time to produce a kind of stage activity which will no longer permit the masses to be silent spectators which will . . . allow them to fuse with the action on the stage . . . A thousand-eyed NEW DIRECTOR, equipped with all modern means of understanding and communication.
MOHOLY-NAGY, *Theatre, Circus, Variety* (1924)

Notes on OPTIGRAPH #3/Berlin Read-out
A machine stands mute beneath the rubble of the now defunct wall. At one time useful in surveillance of the FRONTIER, it now lies exposed and vulnerable. Architecture too is suspended here in this trench, mutilated and beheaded. All around are monoliths, displaced and ridiculous, immersed in a sea of concrete and steel. The mechanism's precise instruments are useless underneath this dense shrapnel. Lenses, dials and other implements of perfection make up this absurd mechanism. What architecture is this curious equipment capable of embodying? You suspect the terrain this mechanism once incised to be embellished with PARA-AXIAL RAYS AND PENCILS. A screen set in position prepares the territory for surveying. Data is randomly propelled from the terminal in search of other DEDICATED LINES. A constant bombardment, a relentless din of fact arises from the interminable void beneath the screen. Distant objects strewn along the landscape are monitored, received as signals, converted to tones, then relayed on. Information is processed continually and deciphered for latent constructs. An obscure text is written and displayed on screen by activating the 'Wave Horn.' Less detectable emissions collide with particles that are all ready in flight. These imperceptible battles result in slight distortions of the encircling space. Every procedure and adjustment made remains etched in the picture plane. The space that results within this void is fluid and malleable. Any attempt to lock on a specific read-out would only result in an abrupt SYSTEM CRASH. Two spheres of equal dimension travelling towards each other at an incalculable speed appear on the screen. The eventual termination of these converging trajectories may never transpire, however the mere possibility generates a multiplicity of unfolding events. The ever decreasing distance between the two bodies forms an endless array of number sequences.

MOSCOW THEATRE, HERMITAGE GARDENS, MOSCOW

The orbits are mapped according to interval readings. The quantity of light waves present is constantly monitored by a simple device known as an interferometer. The mount carrying this instrument is moved backwards away from a micrometer scale until its own image appears on the screen. The scale utilised falls within the region of the first focal plane, the objective. All relevant crosswires are adjusted accordingly in order to determine the mean value. THE ILLUMINATION CURVE is significant as various elements infiltrate the field without cause. Changes in the text conform to an oscillating horizon line and are promptly transferred onto lead sheets. EXPERIMENTAL STUDY OF FRINGES AND OTHER UNCHARTED ZONES; the unused or better, ill-used modules are installed. A zone or territory of wonder uncovered within the apparatus is now accessible. It is here that otherwise irrelevant criteria are exploited, thereby deriving the enigmatic CONSTRUCT OF DESIRE. THE LINGERING POSSIBILITIES OF INPUT; a negligible shift in the diffraction pattern is remedied by the DELAY command. THE EFFECT OF FINITE WIDTH; the unremitting commotion of the printer mimics all emblems of order.

THE PRODUCTION OF AN INFINITE OBJECT; method has little importance, as the outcome is ineffectual and irrelevant. Instead ENTER an utterance, not unlike a breath, as a beginning. Once calibrated, commence with this reticent construction of being. The molecular structures forged by the random collisions are immediately transfigured into phenomena. The registration of these combats on a thin plate is only a scrawl, yet its very emergence signifies a becoming. The most relevant findings are the accidental occurrences, typically referred to as coincidental. Often perplexing, these important revelations defy great odds. The spectrum of chance is also subjected to an altered scale, a domain of very large numbers. Here the inconceivable event occurs with increased frequency. Theorems are only deployed to reverse the/absolute/condition. This will sustain you when navigating well trodden streets towards the unanticipated. An undulating line traces an infinite spiral (as if modelling some arcane stair) in the distant perspective. Beneath this optic city the tools and weapons of science are set into the fragile walls. The spherical surface evident on the screen is revealed incrementally. Some facet of its curvilinear terrain is visible just below two unconnected lines. A field enlarged by manoeuvering lenses and deploying ocular ammunition unearths other worthless inventions. Utensils of perfection are scattered throughout the depths, bathed in a purified beam of light. The wave particles that form this ray plummet through diaphragms and apertures, only to expire while suspended in the abyss. The entire volume is relentlessly engraved by other curious instruments of measure and calculation. A residue or 'ghosting effect' results from these inscriptions which erode the metal and glass casings. This precipitation of light carries with it trace elements of undisclosed matter. They are meticulously scrutinised, revealing an array of strange patterns that gyrate through the cavity. Regions not easily reached are the abode of reason. Here the vapours of prior combats make this post impervious to other tentative invasions. Particles that fill these far reaches are complex and unstable, although a minor adjustment will briefly stabilise the configuration. A variety of gears and cogs drive other more delicate mechanisms high above. Mirages of archaic machinery that seem to be projected from somewhere beyond the picture plane inhabit this region. Their elusive simulation is perpetually dissected in an attempt to eliminate all vestiges of the figure, yet the idea of the machine perseveres. The dimension of the OPTIGRAPH is now immeasurable, you are no longer capable of piloting it. The space that it gauges is no longer in the realm of the tangible. The object has been irradiated. You are both inhabitant and prisoner of a city that is the OPTIGRAPH.

OPTIGRAPH #4 /Paris

The Optigraph may be manipulated on site by adjusting its various instruments, thereby revealing a number of resultant architectures for any given area. This particular device is equipped with three 'screens' each varying in scale and range.

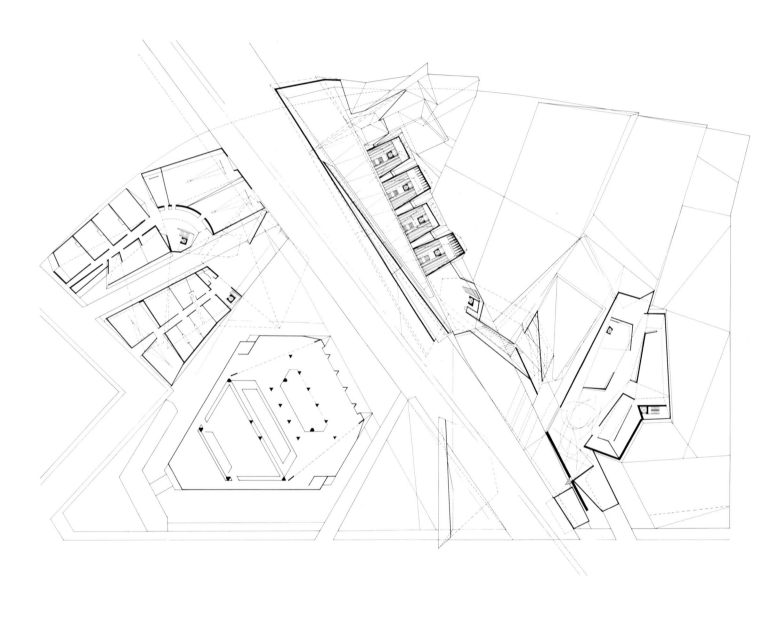

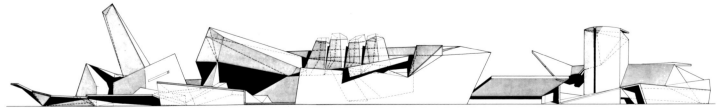

ALEXANDRIA LIBRARY, ALEXANDRIA, EGYPT

SURVEYANCE 001 . . . The Optigraph was placed before the Pont Neuf and in the Place Dauphine on a number of occasions in order to record the ever-changing light and activity. Each reading was retained and collapsed onto the next until the final one was taken from the Seine through screen B. The result is a place reignited from it's colourful history. Amongst the list of functions for this place are the following: fairground, bazaar, an employment exchange, bookstalls, a card factory, a dairy and 'cabinets d'aisance inodores'. The buildings proposed would effectively be attached to the bridge and move towards the Place Dauphine. Here one may partake in any number of activities such as having a tooth pulled, watch a tight rope dancer, buy a Fragonard, pick up a new book or first edition, arrange to go up in a balloon, take fencing lessons or attend a surgical demonstration.

SURVEYANCE 002 . . . A number of readings were taken along the Boulevard du Palais and Rue de la Cité. Eventually the Optigraph was set before the Hotel Dieu, 21 degrees to the north of the Eglise Notre Dame. The architecture that emerged in screen A incorporates a number of uses that are contrary to the present use of the area surrounding Notre Dame. In contrast to the government facilities that now deaden the area this proposal calls for a light manufacturing quarter where wood, bronze, velvet, tin, cotton, paper and china may all be transformed into beautiful objects. In contrast to the judicial and administrative facilities are a number of 'aromatic' dens where every type of furnishing may be produced at the highest possible standard. For these craftsmen would be artists not bureaucrats with a full measure of artist's temperament. Amongst the varieties of furniture produced would be the following: the 'Duchesse' for relaxation, the 'Voyeuse' for watching, the 'Chauffeuse' to facilitate undressing, the 'chaise en confessionel', the 'Confidante' and the 'Tête-à-Tête'.

SURVEYANCE 003 . . . Manipulating the Optigraph from one station point in the Palais de Justice through a 270-degree arc resulted in this proposal. The architecture that remained in screen C surrounds the Sainte Chapelle in a precinct of enlightened curiosity or a place of 'Frontier Incidents'. Amongst other occurences here one may watch private theatrical performances or the frequent arrivals and departures of a variety of airborne machines. Within this place is a exemplary manufacturer of fine velvet and a refuge for dilletante artists. The museum of Automata is also located here with its vast collection. Amongst the items on display are figures that play the flute, beat drums and carry on games of chess. Also one may see an automatic duck that quacks and flaps its wings or an automatic artisan that can produce an endless chain of links.
Hani Rashid

Knowledge is an old error remembering its youth.
Taste is as tiring as well-bred people.
The most beautiful dicovery of man is bicarbonate of soda.
Vegetables are more serious than men and more sensitive in frost.
The world is steeped in good taste and ignorance pasted together.
Painting is made for dentists.
Really, it is only mediocre people who have genius during their lifetime.
It rains and I think of the poor people for whom it doesn't rain.
Human beings win diplomas and lose their instinct.
The more one pleases, the more one displeases.
The only way to have followers is to run faster then the others.
It's easier to scratch one's ass than one's heart (St Augustine).
The unknown is an exception, the known a deception.
A favourable wind has blue feathers.
Tables turn, thanks to the spirit; pictures and other works of art might be called safe-depositables: the spirit is inside and becomes increasingly inspired as the auction prices mount.
Only useless things are indispensable.
FRANCIS PICABIA
'Le Premier Mai'
Literature no 14, June 1920.

CHRISTIAN NORBERG-SCHULZ
THE NEW TRADITION

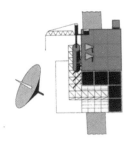

In spite of some resistance Bernard Tschumi has insisted on naming this series of constructs 'follies' because they combine the idea of the 'Folly' in an 18th century English garden, with the kind of madness described by Foucault in his Histoire de la folie.

In his seminal book *Space, Time and Architecture*, S Giedion used as a sub-title 'The growth of a New Tradition', intending that the various currents of Modernism, in spite of their differences, have a common denominator, and that they imply a kind of 'development'.[1] Giedions's belief in the new architecture, however, has more recently been shaken by the so-called 'crisis of the Modern Movement'. It is today an obvious fact that the hopes and expectations offered by Modernism have not been fulfilled. As a result, architecture has to a high extent been marked by short-lived fashions, such as Brutalism, Structuralism, Neo-Rationalism and Post-Modernism. It is therefore about time that we ask whether Giedion's belief in a 'New Tradition' has any foundation.

As a first question, we may ask if it is really possible to combine the words 'new' and 'tradition'. Does not the idea of something *new* contradict the very concept of tradition? Giedion, however, did not use the word 'new' to designate something that has no relationship to the past. In 1944 he wrote: 'Contemporary architecture had to take the hard way. As with painting and sculpture, it had to begin anew. It had to reconquer the most primitive things, as if nothing had ever been done before.'[2] Rather than the creation of something essentially new, Giedion thus wanted a reconquest of the 'most primitive things' were discovered by man. The intention was to establish an alternative to what he called the 'ruling taste' of the 19th century with its 'devaluated symbols'.[3]

Giedion often started his lectures saying: 'I am a pupil of Heinrich Wölfflin'. Here the need to belong to a tradition also comes forth. One might object that Wölfflin did not concern himself with the problems of Modern art and architecture. Certainly not. But he worked out *Grundbegriffe* or 'basic concepts' that, as '*Grund*-begriffe', imply a return to the 'beginning', or in Wölfflin's own words, to the reconquest of 'general forms of perception'.[4] This is not the place to evaluate the basic concepts of Wölfflin; it is only my intention to substantiate that Giedion wanted a general basis for his 'New Tradition'.

It is well known that Wölfflin's method was applied to architecture by his pupil Paul Frankl in the important book *Die Entwicklungsphasen der neueren Architektur*, which was published in English with the title *Principles of Architectural History*.[5] As I once asked Giedion what I should do to improve my understanding of architectural form, he answered: 'You must read Frankl!' In fact I did, and I may assert that Frankl's analyses of buildings from the Renaissance and the Baroque show that the 'most primitive things' are present in any authentic work of architecture.

I may also quote the pioneers of Modern art, to confirm Modernism's search for a general basis. Paul Klee, for instance, wanted to arrive 'where the original laws nourish the development', and he said about himself that he 'dwells close to the heart of creation'.[6] De Chirico wanted to 'return to the basic phenomena of existence', and Brancusi aimed at representing the 'pure and real essence of things'.[7] Max Ernst said about Hans Arp that 'he brings us back to the lost paradise, to the secret of the Universe', and that 'he teaches us to understand again the language spoken by the world itself'.[8] Even the abstract artist *par excellence*, Piet Mondrian, wanted to grasp the basic structures of reality, and defined his art as a 'new realism'. His general aim was to 'unify man with the universe'.[9] These quotations must suffice to prove that the New Tradition does not stem from a nihilistic attitude to what is given, but rather from a return to the 'beginning', as a reaction to the 'ruling taste'.

It is, however, important to emphasise that 'beginning' here does not imply a simple return. The Modern Movement wanted, after all, to be the expression of a new epoch, and Giedion over and over again asserted that our time suffers from its inability to 'control or organise [artistically] the possibilities that it has itself produced.'[10] We may characterise the new epoch or world with the words 'openness' and 'dynamism'. Communication and interaction have replaced isolation and self-sufficiency, and a new 'conception of space' has accordingly come into being. This state of affairs has justly been seen as the origins of Modern art.

But how can we combine 'openness' with the demand for a 'timeless' basis? *That is in fact the decisive question we have to answer, if we want to confirm the idea of a New Tradition.* To start with, we may assert that the unification of openness and beginning implies that something *remains* through all changes. Accordingly, Giedion chose for the 'First Gropius Lecture' at Harvard University 1961 the title 'Constancy and Change', and emphasised in his talk the need for a 'new continuity'.[11] To be able to answer the question, we have, however, to investigate the 'growth' of the New Tradition somewhat closer.

In general, we may distinguish between three phases in the development of Modern art, which we may call *destruction*, *construction* and *movement*. These phases do not constitute a simple temporal succession and may therefore also be understood as simultaneous aspects of a total process. 'Destruction' here means a demolishment of the forms of the past, that is, an abolition of the 'devaluated symbols'. 'Construction' means to establish a new basis through destruction, a basis which may remain in spite of all changes. 'Movement', finally, implies coming to terms with the world by means of construction, in order to do justice to the pluralistic situation of our time.

As we all know, the destruction of the past started with the artistic 'isms' that came into being about and just after the turn of the century. What was abolished, were first of all the historic styles, but also the particular forms or 'figures' which constituted the 'literal' content of conventional art. Van de Velde condemned these forms as 'lies' and Giedion added that 'the past for the moment was dead and had to remain dead'.[12] As a substitute for the styles, Sullivan's slogan *form follows function* was adopted, and as a consequence all conventional forms were 'forbidden'. When I studied architecture during the years after World War II, it was simply not allowed to use sloping roofs, window holes or arches, if one wanted to be 'modern'. In order to give this prohibition a meaning, it was asserted that the styles and the conventional forms were the manifestation of an obsolete 'space conception'.[13]

The destruction of the past was interpreted by Frank Lloyd Wright as the 'destruction of the box',[14] whereby the term 'box' was used as a token of the static and perspective conception of space. Also for Wright, the basic aim was the 'search for the *qualities* in all things'.[15] In our time that means 'welcoming spaciousness as a modern human need', and thus to see the 'building not as a cave but as broad shelter in the open . . .'[16]

It is here not possible to follow the history of destruction in more detail; I just want to recall that the first aim of the Bauhaus was to 'free' the student from his inhibitions, that is, from all 'known' forms. This aim was still the point of departure for Moholy-Nagy when in 1939 he founded the Institute of Design in Chicago.[17] And I may add that destruction is back again today in the guise of Deconstructionism, a current to which I shall return later.

For the growth of the New Tradition destruction is necessary, but only as a condition for a *construction* that aims at the establishment of a new basis. The hope that this aim would be satisfied by Sullivan's slogan, however, has not been fulfilled. Forms do not 'follow' from functions, at least not when the word 'follow' is understood in terms of causality. It is in fact one of the basic misunderstandings of Modernism that the relationship between function and form is one of cause and effect.

From *destruction*, however, form 'followed', that offered the promise of a new 'beginning'. One might in this context mention numerous achievements, such as the new interpretation of the acts of standing and opening in the iron-and-glass architecture of the 19th century.[18] Particularly important was Frank Lloyd Wright's transformation of the box into a juxtaposition of vertical and horizontal planes or slabs. Thereby the *plan libre*, or 'open plan', became possible, and the New Tradition had obtained its first basic principle. The importance of Wright's early works is proved by their influence on European architecture after his opus was published in Germany in 1911. It is Giedion's merit to have explained the significance of the plane in Modern art and architecture as a manifestation of the new conception of space.[19] And it was also him who discovered its historical background.

The logical consequences of Wright's destruction were drawn by Le Corbusier in his 'Five points to a new architecture'.[20] Here the first deliberate construction of the New Tradition was carried out, and the new conception of space was related to the 'most primitive things'. That is, the relationship of the building to the earth, to the sky, and to the horizon were interpreted anew by Le Corbusier by means of the *pilotis*, the *roof garden*, and the *free facade*, as aspects of the superior principle of the *free plan*. Le Corbusier himself said: 'The five points imply a fundamentally new aesthetic. Nothing of the architecture of former epochs remain . . .'[21] Certainly; but the reconquest of the 'most primitive things' was accomplished!

Whereas Le Corbusier at the outset concentrated his attention on the reinterpretation of basic spatial relation-

ships, the Bauhaus aimed at the development of a 'new sensibility' towards materials and forms. The point of departure was the belief that 'any human action and expression consists of components that are determined by man's biological constitution', to quote Moholy-Nagy.[22] Accordingly the *basic course* started with 'tactile exercises' which aimed at an 'experiential understanding of the material' as an initiation for grasping the 'totality of life'.[23] Again, thus, we encounter the conviction that everything in the world possesses basic properties, which we have to 'reconquer' after their 'devaluation' during the 19th century. We ought to notice, however, that Moholy-Nagy conceived the totality in terms of its subordinate components, in contrast to Le Corbusier's more global approach.

The 'atomistic' attitude which predominated at the Bauhaus culminated with the book *Language of Vision* by the former Bauhaus student Gyorgy Kepes. Here we read: 'We live in the midst of a whirlwind of light qualities. From this whirling confusion we build unified entities, those forms of experience called visual images. . . . Nature forms; flowers, trees, rocks, mountains, cloud formations, animal or human bodies as well as man-made forms; buildings or implements, are only temporary configurations in the perpetual flux of becoming and disappearing.'[24] But Kepes does not explain *how* we are able to recognise a 'temporary configuration' *as something*. How do we 'build a unified entity' or an 'image' out of a 'whirling confusion'? 'Through experience' Kepes says. But on which basis does experience start? Evidently the task is impossible, if we do not *in advance* possess a notion of the things mentioned. Kepes must have felt this, when he added: 'Every form is a visible record of *origin*.'[25] Again, thus, we encounter the problem of 'constancy and change'.

For a long time one believed that the New Tradition might grow on the basis of Le Corbusier's Five Points and the New Sensibility of the Bauhaus. Already in 1944, however, Giedion realised that something was lacking, and wrote: 'In countries where modern architecture has won the battle and been entrusted with monumental tasks involving more than functional problems, one cannot but observe that something is lacking in the buildings executed. This something is an inspired architectural imagination able to satisfy the demand for monumentality.'[26] The 'dangerous' word 'monumentality' he defined as: 'Monumentality springs from the eternal need of people to create symbols for their activities and for their fate or destiny, for their religious beliefs and for their social convictions.'[27] Then he added: 'Every period has the impulse to the create symbols in the form of monuments, which, according to the Latin meaning are things that remind, things to be transmitted to later generations.'[28] Giedion extends the concept of 'tradition' to comprise a new dimension of *meaning*, and he suggests that architecture can only become *meaningful* through a new relationship with the temporality of human life.

Giedion carried this on in two essays, which at the beginning of 1954 were published in the American magazine *Architectural Record* under the common heading 'The State of Contemporary architecture'. Their titles were: 'The Regional Approach' and 'The Need for Imagination'. The need for imagination was, according to Giedion, satisfied by Le Corbusier's last works, above all the pilgrimage church at Ronchamp, which Giedion praised as a 'symbol of the inner strivings of our period, a courageous recognition of the present' . . . 'the oldest and the newest as being borne within it'.[29] The regional approach, which ought to bring forth a 'new regionalism' that 'satisfies both cosmic

As a result of the unlikely co-operation between Peter Eisenman and Jacques Derrida; Joyce's garden is intentionally self-referential, with architectural as well as literary associations that simultaneously relate to the past, present and future.

Aldo Rossi believes that architecture, which is typically conceived in isolation, thrives on the life and history of the city when it is placed within it, but is contradicted by it at the same time. The Ossuary of Modena, which dominates a city of the dead suffers no such contradiction.

and terrestrial conditions',[30] was already latent in the works of Frank Lloyd Wright, and then realised in a particularly convincing way in the 'Finnish Modern' of Alvar Aalto. Thus Giedion writes: 'Finland is with Aalto wherever he goes. It provides him with that inner source of energy, which always flows through his work. It is as Spain is to Picasso or Ireland to James Joyce.'[31] What Finland means, he describes with these words: 'Finland, covered with its network of lakes and forest, suggests in its structure the days of the Creation, when water and earth were first separated.'[32] We understand, thus, that the aim again is the 'reconquest of the most primitive things'! (I may add that this problem occupied Giedion to the very end; his last books in fact concentrate on the relationship between 'beginning and change'.[33])

With the reconquest of the dimensions of Monumentality and Regionalism, the New Tradition gained a comprehensive scope. Although a direction had been indicated, however, the problem of meaning was not solved. In fact, the *movement* came to a standstill about 1960, and has later not found its track again. During the last decades we have rather experienced an incessant succession of fashions, none of which have offered a true contribution to the New Tradition. Certainly there have been exceptions, but the implicit movement has not been able to take the lead. Before we consider these exceptions, we must, however, ask why the great promise of the post-war years was not fulfilled.

Many reasons of a practical, economic and artistic nature may be indicated, but rather than entering into these complex matters, I shall ask whether the New Tradition itself became the victim of an 'inner' weakness. In my opinion it did, and more precisely I may assert that it lost its momentum because the contradiction between constancy and change was never solved. *Here I see the deeper reason for the crisis of Modern architecture.*

According to Giedion, the basic aim of Modernism was to heal the 'split of thought and feeling' that has characterised Western civilisation since Descartes.[34] At the Bauhaus an attempt was made to unify the two through a pseudo-scientific approach, understanding everything as an organisation of atomistic elements. This approach, however, implies a confusion of 'feeling' and 'sensibility'; since the former is related to meaningful wholes rather than separate stimuli. The goal of the Bauhaus was a comprehensive *Gesamtkunstwerk*, but the attempt to arrive at this goal from 'below' could not succeed. We could also say that one did not really proceed beyond the phase of destruction.

The atomistic approach is repeated today by the so-called 'Deconstructionists' such as Tschumi and Eisenman, who, because of our seemingly hopeless situation, let the architectural endeavour dissolve into an outspoken *nihilism*. Thus Tschumi writes: ' . . . today's cultural circumstances suggest the need to discard established categories of meaning and contextual histories, . . . to encourage conflict over synthesis, fragmentation over unity, madness and play over careful management, . . . [aiming] at an architecture that *means nothing*.'[35] The 'method' employed Tschumi indicates with these words:' . . . my pleasure has never surfaced in looking at buildings . . . but rather in dismantling them.'[36]

Evidently, Deconstructionism represents a reaction to the static 'typologies' introduced after 1960 by the Neo-Rationalists, such as Aldo Rossi.[37] Here we return to quasi-academic compositions which abandon the basic modern achievement of the *plan libre*. The aim is a return to 'gener-

ally understood' forms, that is, another manifestation of the wish for a reconquest of the 'most primitive things'. In general, the New Rationalism and Deconstructionism represent the aspects of constancy and change respectively, without, however, bringing about a synthesis that may heal the split of thought and feeling. Neither of them therefore deserves the label 'modern', since they depart from the basic aim of the New Tradition.

Does this state of affairs imply that the contradiction between constancy and change *cannot* be solved, and that the reconquest of the 'most primitive things' is impossible in our open and dynamic time? At any rate, we have to conclude that the solution so far offered by the Modern Movement has not been satisfactory. When the problem of *meaning in architecture* came forth,[38] it was unable to offer a coherent theory, although certain successful works were realised. The reason for this failure is undoubtedly that the pioneers of Modernism were caught up by European idealism, and understood 'constancy' or 'origin' in terms of *idea* or *Ding an sich*. That is, they approached the problem of constancy as the recurrence of absolute forms on the basis of a utopian wish for unity and harmony. Giedion's 'constituent facts' are such ideal entities that 'always recur'.[39] The pseudo-scientific approach of the Bauhaus did not solve the problem, and the later currents have, as suggested before, stressed only one of the two aspects at the expense of the other. Hence Modernism remained an 'unfinished project'.[40] I may conclude that it is impossible to unify constancy and change, as long as we understand what remains in terms of *idea* or *Ding ans sich*.

Is there any way out of this dilemma? My answer is *yes*, and more precisely, the solution is offered by the thinking of Martin Heidegger. It may perhaps seem strange to use Heidegger, who is considered a conservative, to overcome the crisis of Modern art and architecture. It is a fact, however, that Heidegger carried out a liberating destruction of European metaphysics, which corresponds to the destruction by Modernism of the devaluated symbols of the past. In addition he accomplished a *construction*, which opens up a new way towards meaning, that is, a way which serves an open and dynamic world. In general, he no longer understands the 'Being of beings' in terms of *Ding an sich*, but rather as a *Seinsweise* or mode of 'being-in-the-world'.[41] A being, thus, is no longer considered a 'shadow' of an absolute idea, but gains its identity from how it is related to other beings, or in Heidegger's words, how it participates in the 'mirror-play of the world'.[42]

In his *magnum opus Sein und Zeit* from 1927, Heidegger carried out an analysis of man's being in the world as *Dasein*, and in later writings he has investigated the *Seinsweise* of other beings. In his essay on 'The Thing' he uses the jug as a major example, and in 'Building Dwelling Thinking' he offers a description of the bridge. Here we read: 'The bridge swings over the stream with ease and power. It does not just connect banks that are already there. The banks emerge as banks only as the bridge crosses the stream. The bridge designedly causes them to lie across from each other. One side is set off against the other by the bridge. Nor do the banks stretch along the stream as indifferent border strips of the dry land. With the banks, the bridge bring to the stream the one and the other expanse of the landscape lying behind them. It brings stream and bank and land into its other's neighbourhood. The bridge *gathers* the earth as landscape around the stream.'[43] This description shows us what Heidegger intends with the term 'being-in-the-world'. Here the bridge emerges as part of or participant in a world, and its meaning is understood in terms of this participation. At the same time other participants, such as the stream, the banks, and the land, emerge as what they are.

The difference from a scientific description which concentrates its attention on 'components' rather than relationships, is evident. Heideggger himself characterises his procedure as *phenomenology*, and says that 'phenomenology is the science of the Being of entities'.[44] His point of departure was Husserl's battle-cry 'Back to the things themselves', but whereas Husserl understood things in terms of human consciousness, Heidegger really approached them as such, by investigating their being-in-the-world.[45] It is not possible here to offer a further look into the problems of phenomenology; I only want to emphasise that the 'method' implies a return to the phenomena and problems of our daily life-world in the light of the 'most primitive things', overcoming thus the abstractions of the sciences. The Being of the live-world Heidegger defines as a 'Fourfold of Earth and Sky, Mortals and Divinities.'[46]

In general, Heidegger shows that origin or beginning has to be understood in terms of being-in-the-world, and that any *Seinsweise* or mode is open to ever new interpretations and manifestations. His 'construction' is therefore eminently *dynamic*, and makes the contradiction between constancy and change disappear. Thus he shows how we must intend the *movement* of the New Tradition.

Evidently Modernism aimed at a 'grounded dynamism' of this kind, but its realisation was hindered by conventional metaphysics. Above all it was hindered by the late-metaphysical approach of modern science, which reduces everything to what is 'measurable'. An interesting example is offered by the preoccupation of several of the pioneers with Einstein's Theory of Relativity. The term 'space-time', thus, often appears in writings of Modern art, and is also reflected in the very title of Giedion's famous book.[47] The reference may have a certain validity, since the Theory of Relativity and Modern art are both concerned with the understanding of a world which is intended as open and dynamic. It has to be emphasised, however, that Modern art is not determined by modern physics, but, as ever before, by man's daily life-world. Through phenomenology it becomes possible to understand this world in the true sense of the word: as a 'standing under' or among the things. Thus we are ready to realise Moholy-Nagy's battle-cry: 'Design for life'.[48]

My criticism of the pseudo-scientific approach of the pioneers of Modernism does not imply that they did not contribute to the movement of the New Tradition. We may rather say that the pioneers in reality were phenomenologists who did not, however, understand the true nature of their work. And we may add that art in general may be considered an 'applied phenomenology'. Phenomenology and art are both concerned with meaning, the first as a 'bringing-into-word', the second as a 'setting-into-work'. Hence phenomenology heals the split between thinking and feeling. The failure of the Modern Movement in fact shows that thinking and feeling, or theory and practice, belong together, and that the movement stops when they fall apart. Through the unity of pure and applied phenomenology, the New Tradition may find the track again, and realise the 'grounded dynamism' intended at the outset.

It remains to ask whether significant contributions to the movement are already present. Again it is Giedion's merit to have discovered the first manifestations. I have already recalled his praise of the works of Alvar Aalto, as an example of the New Regionalism. In the last edition of *Space, Time and Architecture* from 1967 he furthermore added a chapter entitled 'Jörn Utzon and the Third Generation', where he pointed out that some younger architects profess a 'new relation to the past', which implies a 'right of expression above pure function'.[49] Thus he finds in the works of Utzon an ability to 'have direct contact with the cosmic elements of nature and the past and also complete control of contemporary methods of industrialised production, especially prefabrication. As a result he is able to detach prefabrication from its purely mechanistic attributes and bring it nearer to the organic.'[50] It may be added that Utzon also expresses the *genius loci*, and thus satisfies the demand for symbolic as well as regional qualities, without relapsing into the imitation of stylistic motifs.

I cannot here discuss the works of other exponents of the 'third generation', but have to recall the fundamental contribution of Louis Kahn, who more than anybody else reconquered the phenomenological understanding of architecture, and even at a time when the 'crisis' of Modernism came forth, that is, about 1960. Kahn's question: 'What does the building want to be?' implies that he neither intended ideal form nor meaningless deconstruction, but that he took the being-in-the-world of each task as his point of departure. In an article in *Oppositions* 1979, I pointed out the basic correspondence between Kahn's approach and Heidegger's thinking, and showed how both understood the building as a 'gathering of a world'.[51] Kahn's preoccupation with 'beginnings' and his distinction between 'form' and 'design' also prove that he came very close to the 'grounded dynamism' explained before. His collected writings were in fact published under the title 'What will be has always been'.[52] Kahn's written statements, however, remain fragmentary, and need the phenomenology of Heidegger to become a coherent theory. On the other hand, the works of Kahn serve to illustrate how Heidegger's thinking may release the movement of the New Tradition.

Kahn's successors only to a certain degree understood his message. Robert Venturi, thus, aims at a true dynamism, but often ends up with a composition of 'conventional forms', rather than a new interpretation of 'what has always been'. Unfortunately this fallacy became the mark of innumerable works of Post-Modernism, which in many cases look even more superficial than the devaluated symbols of the 19th century.[53] It ought to be added, however, that Post-Modernism brought to our attention the problem of meaning in architecture and the need for a contemporary 'language' of forms, or rather, it reminded us of the fact that the language of architecture in addition to the organisation of space, also has to comprise the dimensions of 'built form' and 'typology'.

The New Tradition initiated its movement with a new definition of spatial organisation, as indicated by Le Corbusier's *plan libre*. A certain development of this concept has later taken place, as well as relapses into more static modes of composition. The built form was given less attention at the outset, and mostly reduced to a question of 'sensibility' to materials and textures. More significant aspects of the dimension were brought to our attention after World War II, for instance in Le Corbusier's later works. The dimension of typology, finally, was practically forgotten until the event of Louis Kahn and Post-Modernism. Being a particularly difficult aspect of the architectural totality, it demands a careful distinction between imitation and interpretation, whereby 'type' is understood as a *Seinsweise* rather than an ideal form.

Venturi and Scott Brown have successfully balanced a consistently literary, theoretical discourse with an empirical sociology that has been expressed in both individual buildings and planning proposals.

Summing up, I may assert that the concept of a New Tradition remains valid. It has gone through several phases of destruction and construction; phases that in part have remained hidden, that is, concealed behind the more apparent currents of Brutalism, Structuralism, Post-Modernism, Neo-Rationalism and Deconstructionism. And still, a *growth* has taken place. Whether the movement may continue depends on our ability to adopt a phenomenological attitude, intending wholes and inter-relationships rather than single facts. The Deconstructionists are right in maintaining that ideologies and systems belong to the past. They are mistaken, however, when they conclude that the present world is meaningless. But meaning can only be realised if we understand and respect the modes of being-in-the-world which distinguish every entity that exists. To arrive at such an understanding is the same as the 'reconquest of the most primitive things', or in Heidegger's words, the reconquest of *Being*. Only in this way may we leave the 'crisis of Modernism' behind, and resume the movement of the New Tradition.

Notes

1 S Giedion, *Space, Time and Architecture*, Cambridge, Mass, 1941 (1967).
2 S Giedion, *Architecture, You and Me*, Cambridge, Mass, 1958, p 26.
3 S Giedion, *op cit*, p 3.
4 H Wölfflin, *Gedanken zur Kunstgeschichte*, Basel, 1940, p 7ff.
5 P Frankl, *Principles of Architectural History*, Cambridge, Mass, 1968.
6 C Giedion-Welcker, *Schriften 1926-1971*, Köln, 1973, pp 342, 347.
7 *op cit*, pp 387, 388.
8 *op cit*, p 259.
9 P Mondrian, *Plastic Art and Pure Plastic Art*, New York, 1945, p 17.
10 S Giedion, *op cit*, p 6.
11 S Giedion, *Constancy, Change and Architecture*, Cambridge, Mass, 1961.
12 S Giedion, *Architecture, You and Me*, p 28.
13 Compare with the 'rules' introduced by Arnold Schoenberg for the 'destruction' of tonality. A Schoenberg, *Style and Idea*, New York, 1951.
14 F L Wright, *The Natural House*, New York, 1970, p 34.
15 *op cit*, p 15.
16 *op cit*, p 16.
17 L Moholy-Nagy, *Vision in Motion*, Chicago, 1947, p 65.
18 S Giedion, *Space, Time and Architecture*, p 271ff.
19 *op cit*, p 413.
20 Le Corbusier, *Oeuvre Complète 1910-1929*, Zürich 1937, p 128. Also A Roth, *Zwei Wohnhäuser von Le Corbusier und Pierre Jeanneret*, Stuttgart, 1927, pp 6ff.
21 A Roth, *op cit*.
22 L Moholy-Nagy, *Von Material zu Architecktur*, München, 1929, p 8.
23 *op cit*, p 17.
24 G Kepes, *Language of Vision*, Chicago, 1948, p 15.
25 *op cit*, p 186.
26 S Giedion, *Architecture, You and Me*, p 32.
27 *op cit*, p 28.
28 *op cit*, p 28.
29 *op cit*, p 196.
30 *op cit*, p 149.
31 S Giedion, *Space, Time and Architecture*, p 620.
32 *op cit*, p 622.
33 S Giedion, *The Eternal Present; The Beginnings of Art and The Beginnings of Architecture*, New York, 1962, 1964.
34 S Giedion, *Architecture, You and Me*, p 72.
35 B Tschumi, 'Parc de la Villette', *Architectural Design* 3/4, 1988.
36 B Tschumi, *Disjunctions*, Berlin, 1987.
37 A Rossi, *L'architettura della città*, Padova, 1966.
38 C Norberg-Schulz, 'Meaning in Architecture' in C Jencks, G Baird (eds), *Meaning in Architecture*, London, 1969.
39 The same may be said about Michael Graves' 'figural' elements.
40 The expression stems from Jürgen Habermas.
41 M Heidegger, *Grundfragen der Philosophie*, Frankfurt, 1984, p 24.
42 M Heidegger, 'The Thing' in *Poetry, Language, Thought*, New York, 1971.
43 M Heidegger, 'Building Dwelling Thinking' in *Poetry, Language, Thought*, New York, 1971, p 152.
44 M Heidegger, *Being and Time*, New York, 1962, p 61.
45 F W Von Herrmann, *Der Begriff der Phänomenologie bei Heidegger und Husserl*, Frankfurt, 1981.
46 M Heidegger, 'Building Dwelling and Thinking', p 150.
47 S Georgiadis, *Sigfried Giedion, eine intellektuelle Biographie*, Zürich, 1989, makes the problem a major issue.
48 L Moholy-Nagy, *Vision in Motion*, pp 33ff.
49 S Giedion, *Space, Time and Architecture*, pp 668ff.
50 *op cit*, p 678.
51 C Norberg-Schulz, 'Kahn, Heidegger and the Language of Architecture' in *Oppositions* 18, Cambridge, Mass, 1980.
52 R S Wurman, *What will be has always been. The Words of Louis I Kahn*, New York, 1986.
53 C Jencks, *The Language of Post-Modern Architecture*, Academy Editions, London, 1977.